# Diversity
# in the
# Classroom

## A Multicultural Approach
## to the Education
## of Young Children

# EARLY CHILDHOOD EDUCATION SERIES

MILLIE ALMY, *Editor*

Elinor Fitch Griffin, *Island of Childhood: Education in the Special World of Nursery School*

Sandra R. Curtis, *The Joy of Movement in Early Childhood*

Frances E. Kendall, *Diversity in the Classroom: A Multicultural Approach to the Education of Young Children*

# Diversity
# in the
# Classroom

## A Multicultural Approach
## to the Education
## of Young Children

FRANCES E. KENDALL

Teachers College, Columbia University
New York and London   1983

*This book is dedicated to the women of the National Student YWCA and the National YWCA. It was with them that I joined "the struggle for peace and justice, freedom and dignity for all people" (YWCA Purpose, 1970). My life has never been the same, and I am immensely grateful.*

Published by Teachers College Press, 1234 Amsterdam Avenue, New York, N.Y. 10027

Library of Congress Cataloging in Publication Data

Kendall, Frances E.
   Diversity in the classroom.

   Includes bibliographies and index.
   1. Intercultural education—United States.
I.  Title.
LC1099.K46   1983        370.19′6        83-6704


ISBN 0-8077-2740-7


All photographs courtesy of *The Children's Advocate*, Berkeley, California. Photographs on pages 11, 19, 38, 42, 50, 59, and 71 by Deborah Shwartz. Photograph on page 33 by Chris Cleary.


Manufactured in the United States of America

88   87                    4   5   6

# Contents

FOREWORD     vii

PREFACE     xi

ACKNOWLEDGMENTS     xiv

1. Toward Multicultural Education     1

2. Understanding Child Development     6
    The Preschool Child     7
    Learning Styles     12
    The Development of Racial Awareness and Racial Attitudes     19

3. Presenting Multicultural Education to Parents     22
    Examining Our Racial Attitudes     22
    Talking with Parents About Multicultural Education     27

4. Preparing for Multicultural Education in the Classroom     30
    Theoretical Basis for a Multicultural Perspective     30
    Guidelines for Dealing with Race in the Classroom     32
    Levels of Involvement in Multicultural Education     36

5. Planning a Resource Unit on Affirming Cultural Diversity     41
    Introduction of the Concept     42
    *Main Idea*     43
    *Organizing Ideas*     43
    *Skills to Be Developed*     43
    *Attitudes and Values to Be Developed*     44
    Unit Plan     44
    Evaluation     56

6. Developing a Multicultural Classroom Environment    58
     Language Arts    58
     Social Studies    62
     Unit Blocks    64
     Dramatic Play    67
     Music and Games    69
     Cooking    72
     Evaluating the Classroom Environment    75

EPILOGUE: Beyond the Classroom    76

APPENDIX A. Bibliography of Multicultural Children's Books    81
APPENDIX B. Bibliography on Institutional Racism    92
APPENDIX C. Sources for Multicultural Materials    98
     Aids for Multicultural Curriculum Development    98
     Resource Centers for Multicultural Materials    99
APPENDIX D. Multicultural Classroom Environment Checklist    102

REFERENCES    105

INDEX    109

# Foreword

In a midwest college last year a young woman student majoring in early childhood education conferred with her adviser about her schedule for the following semester. "This would be a good time to take the course on multicultural approaches," said the adviser. The student shook her head, "I won't need that. I expect I'll get a job near my parents' home. The people in our neighborhood come from very similar backgrounds."

The adviser hesitated. The words, "I never realized that you are so disadvantaged" came to his mind, but instead he said, "The course is required for *all* early childhood majors. When you've been in it for a few sessions, come and see me and we'll discuss how it may be useful for you."

*Diversity in the Classroom: A Multicultural Approach to the Education of Young Children* addresses the nature of cultural diversity in the United States and its implications for developing early childhood curriculum and for teaching young children. It is directed to students and teachers who, like the young woman just described, have never weighed the consequences of prejudice, discrimination, and racism for those people who believe themselves to be isolated from diversity. *Diversity in the Classroom* is also directed to those who have already made some commitment to understanding cultures different from their own and to seeing that young children benefit from the diversity that is so typical of our society.

For both groups Dr. Kendall insists that one only begins to understand others after one comes to terms with one's own experience with and attitudes toward difference. This theme of self-

examination pervades the book. It is an essential first step in learning to observe children. The teacher cannot see the child as an
individual, rather than as a reflection of some cultural stereotype,
until this step has been taken. Self-examination is equally important for establishing good relations with parents and for developing
a multicultural classroom environment.

Self-awareness is necessary but not sufficient for an effective
multicultural approach to early education. What the teacher does
also is derived from knowledge: knowledge of children's development and learning, knowledge of the ways attitudes and values are
acquired, knowledge of different cultures.

Dr. Kendall's succinct description of this knowledge relies heavily on the research and writing of Barbara Biber and her colleagues
for the area of child development and the curriculum. It also draws
on the work of Hilda Taba and her colleagues for "a philosophy of
education for human relations." An extensive list of references and a
rather comprehensive annotated bibliography supplement this description. Dr. Kendall's assertion that multicultural education represents "a new approach" is underscored by the fact that over half
of the works cited date from 1970 to 1981. It may be noted, however, that a number of authors cited, and particularly Taba and
Biber, were actively involved in classrooms, testing out intergroup
approaches to human relations, at least as early as the 1940s.
Readers may like to know that the "new approach" is undergirded
by some four decades of classroom experience. What seems most
noteworthy to me is not so much the newness of the approach, but
rather, as Dr. Kendall also emphasizes, its crucial importance for all
children in today's times.

In addition to this theoretical background, Dr. Kendall provides
two chapters, plus two appendices, that offer specific help for planning a unit on the affirmation of cultural diversity and for planning
a classroom environment that imparts such affirmation. The "how
to" emphasis in these chapters reflects Dr. Kendall's basic respect
for the intelligence, ingenuity, and individuality of teachers as well
as of children.

Teachers, depending not only on their individuality but also on
their situations, will develop multicultural education at different
levels. If, over time, they move from one level to the next, so that
eventually many have integrated multicultural materials and activi-

ties into the curriculum and others have succeeded in making cultural diversity a positive factor in all classroom experience, *Diversity in the Classroom* will have achieved a considerable portion of its author's purpose. Fuller realization of that purpose depends on teachers moving on to becoming agents for change in their schools and communities. Their aspiration? Social justice for children. Not an "impossible dream" but one worth working for.

—Millie Almy, Professor Emerita
University of California, Berkeley

# Preface

I began my formal work on the elimination of racism when I joined the National Student YWCA in 1966. However, because I grew up in the South, the question of race has always been an integral part of my life. I was raised in an upper-middle-class Southern environment; my family was very proud of its gentility and lack of prejudice. No one ever said "nigger." "Nigger," in fact, was one of the four forbidden words in our house—the others being "lie," "cheat," and "steal." Few derogatory comments were made about black people; it just wasn't done. On the other hand, though never really articulated, the rules for interacting with people of color were very clear: "they" came in the back door, sat in the back seat of the car, ate in the kitchen with kitchen silverware, and were given uniforms to wear that acted as a visible sign of their positions. In spite of the fact that I was the child and they were the adults, they addressed me as "Ma'am" or "Miss Francie." I don't remember ever being told these rules or thinking they were at all strange; they were the expected behaviors. When I was eight years old, my mother hired a new maid, a black woman who was only twelve years older than I. As happens in so many Southern homes, she became the significant adult in my life, and the rules that I had always lived by began to make less and less sense.

I left the South when I was thirteen to go away to boarding school. During my high school years I spent increasingly little time at home, thinking that if I absented myself geographically I could leave my history behind. I was horrified by the information that my great grandparents had owned slaves and also by the fact that my family was in the cotton business—a business that was built on the backs of people who benefitted little from their labor. Although it never occurred to me that the racial prejudice I was so keenly aware of in my family had anything to do with my own actions, I carried the burden of guilt for my entire family's behavior. Somehow it was incumbent on me to right all of their moral wrongs.

It wasn't until I began to work with the campus YWCA at the University of Denver that I realized that I too was prejudiced. I saw that I was guilty of perpetuating the racism for which I so condemned my family, simply by continuing to eat at a country club that excluded people of color from its membership or continuing to sit quietly while offensive jokes were told about black people. I wasn't sure I could do anything to change the racial attitudes of my family, though I certainly spent a lot of energy on it, but it became clearer that I could make changes in my own attitudes and behavior. Through enormous struggle and pain (on my part) and endless patience and willingness to trust that white people could change (on the part of women of color in the YWCA), I was able to reaffirm my Southernness, particularly in regard to the ways in which that heritage made me more sensitive to problems and issues of race. In the context of my work in the National Student YWCA, I became committed to working toward "the elimination of racism wherever it exists and by any means necessary."[1] And thus began the work that forms the basis of this book.

When I began graduate work at Bank Street College, New York City, in 1970, one of my goals was to write a curriculum manual focusing on antiracism work in the classroom; I wanted to design a model for enabling children to see themselves as change agents. Although it became clear that I had to narrow my focus for a master's-level thesis, I did begin to combine my commitment to working toward eliminating racism and my interest in early childhood education through two projects. I worked with another student on designing a curriculum unit on growth and change that presented the concept of change as a positive one for children. And I wrote my master's thesis on the use of children's books to reinforce nonracist behavioral patterns in children.

---

[1] The YWCA's One Imperative, adopted at the Twenty-fifth National Convention of the YWCA of the U.S.A., April 1970, Houston, Texas.

After leaving Bank Street, I taught at a demonstration day-care center in Brooklyn, working with three-, four-, five-, and six-year-olds from a variety of racial and ethnic backgrounds. The multitudinous problems of putting an antiracist curriculum into effect in a classroom were immediately apparent; I spent much of the next two years designing a realistic approach to my objective. Unwilling to put off the writing of this curriculum any longer, I entered a doctoral program at the University of North Carolina for the primary purpose of creating an early childhood curriculum that was antiracist in nature.

The chronicling of these events is important because it reflects my approach to multicultural education. I began working on racism first and then chose early childhood education as an arena in which to do that work. Hence in this book I have focused not only on classroom activities but also on the attitudes of the adults who interact with the children. Further, I have addressed not only the development of children's racial attitudes but also the relationship between an individual teacher's racial attitudes and institutional racism. At the heart of *Diversity in the Classroom* is the assumption that these two aspects of multicultural education—teachers' racial attitudes and a multicultural classroom environment—cannot be separated if our goal is positive, growth-producing education for all children.

# Acknowledgments ────────────

Throughout the various stages of this book, I have received enormous support from friends and loved ones, colleagues, and support staff. Writing a book is clearly not a single-handed proposition. To Beverley Simmons and Della Coulter I give my greatest love and appreciation. Each in her own way has given time, energy, care, and concern to this project. To Ann Benjamin I owe tremendous thanks for her tireless researching, her fine thinking, and her willingness to enter someone else's process in its final stages. A panel of five experts in the field of child development, curriculum development, and antiracism did both formative and final evaluations of the first draft of the manuscript; I thank Beryle Banfield, Barbara Biber, Pat Bidol, Edna Shapiro, and Reginald Wilson for their work. I thank the support staff at the Eliot-Pearson Department of Child Study, Tufts University, for their help: Rose Chioccariello, Louise Clancy, Marjorie Manning, Ruth Marotta, Tillie Nelder, and Tina Saunders. Finally, I am very grateful for the enthusiasm, support, and help I have been given by the California contingent: Diane Davenport, Ethel Manheimer, Sayre Van Young, and Deborah Shwartz.

# Diversity
## in the
## Classroom

### A Multicultural Approach
### to the Education
### of Young Children

# Toward Multicultural
# Education _____ 1

Racism is one of the most crippling diseases from which this country suffers. It affects each of us, whether we are white or red, yellow, black, or brown, oppressor or oppressed. Education can be a powerful force in the struggle to eliminate racism. Both adults and children are involved in reaching this goal. As members of the educational system, teachers can work toward the elimination of racism by examining their own roles in the perpetuation of institutional racism. Children, for their part, have the right to experience an affirmation of individual differences and a respect for the cultural heritages of all people. *Diversity in the Classroom: A Multicultural Approach to the Education of Young Children* addresses possible roles for the teacher in the struggle against institutional racism and helps teachers design a curriculum for young children that is multicultural.

This book is based on the developmental-interaction philosophy of education as defined by Shapiro and Biber (1972) and on Hilda Taba's (1955) philosophy of education for human relations. The developmental-interaction philosophy addresses both the cognitive and affective aspects of the child's growth in the design of the education experience. Taba speaks to the importance of working against ethnocentricity in children. The book is also based on the following values regarding the role of the teacher:

> Teachers are models for children; therefore they should show respect and concern for all people.

*1*

Teachers encourage children to explore, to initiate, to question, to grapple with tough questions, and to be active rather than passive learners.

Teachers provide experiences through which children can begin to develop their own values.

Teachers are active participants in children's learning.

Teachers pass their own values and attitudes on to children both intentionally and unintentionally; therefore it is important that they be keenly aware of their own attitudes and values.

The book has two purposes: first, to help teachers identify their own racial attitudes and examine ways in which these attitudes affect their teaching, and second, to help teachers use a multicultural approach to education regardless of the racial or ethnic composition of their classrooms.

Institutional racism in this country reaches beyond the attitudes and actions of the individual. A notorious example of institutional racism in education was the segregation of public schools before the *Brown* v. *Board of Education* decision by the United States Supreme Court in 1954. Prior to *Brown*, the segregation of black children and the maintenance of dual educational institutions were legal even though separate schools were, as the Supreme Court ruled in *Brown*, "inherently unequal." Black people were subordinated on the basis of color, and the legal and educational institutions supported and reinforced unequal treatment.

The manifestations of institutional racism within schools today are subtler than the blatant de jure segregation abolished by the *Brown* decision ("Subtle Racism Seen," 1978). As it has become legally—and socially—unacceptable to support overt racism, the attitudes that were responsible for creating such situations have been driven underground. Despite superficial changes in behavior, underlying attitudes frequently remain the same. A situation now exists that encourages change in teachers' behavior without providing support for changes in attitudes. The result may be that teachers are sending children double messages. That is, even though a teacher may be conscientious about providing materials and information about a variety of cultural, ethnic, and racial groups, she or he may believe at some level that some children are incapable of high academic performance due to their race or culture. Thus negative attitudes may show themselves in ways more subtle than segregation but no less destructive. One goal of this book is to encourage teachers to examine their own racial attitudes in light of the struggle against institutional racism.

Much has been written about multicultural education in the past decade, frequently within the context of the work to eliminate racism in society generally. The following statements by Dolce pinpoint the crucial aspects of multicultural education:

> Multiculturalism is not simply a new methodology which can be grafted onto an educational program. The concept of multiculturalism in education is based upon a different view of society than that which presently appears to exist.
>
> Multiculturalism is a reflection of a value system which emphasizes acceptance of behavioral differences deriving from different cultural systems and an active support of the right of such differences to exist. (Dolce, 1973, p. 283)

Current theorists (Banks, 1973; Gay, 1973; Gold, Grant, & Rivlin, 1977; Youngblood, 1979) prescribe a new approach to education, one in which cultural diversity is affirmed and actively supported through a multicultural classroom environment.

Multicultural education has five primary goals: first, to teach children to respect others' cultures and values as well as their own; second, to help all children learn to function successfully in a multicultural, multiracial society; third, to develop a positive self-concept in those children who are most affected by racism—children of color; fourth, to help all children experience both their differences as culturally diverse people and their similarities as human beings in positive ways; and fifth, to encourage children to experience people of diverse cultures working together as unique parts of a whole community.

Young children who live in a multicultural community experience cultural diversity firsthand; it is part of their world. However, three-, four-, and five-year-olds who live in a monocultural setting may have difficulty imagining an alternative world, a community that is different from theirs. In such a monocultural community, the classroom can be both a familiar, comfortable setting for the children and a multicultural environment of experiences, pictures, music, and books pertaining to people with diverse cultural heritages. In a monocultural community, even more than in a multicultural community, it is crucial that teachers present differences among people as positive qualities. As the children in such a community grow older and are better able to deal with specific information about different cultures, the foundation of respect for diversity will have been firmly laid.

The recent impetus for multicultural education came, in part, from the growing awareness of the lack of equal educational opportunities for all children and from the desegregation of public schools during the 1960s (Youngblood, 1979). Today multicultural education is one of the critical issues facing educators. At the heart of this move toward multicultural education is the belief that this new approach can and should permeate every level of the educational process. The multicultural approach to education is not limited to the selection of appropriate, culturally diverse classroom materials. The election of local school board members in an ethnically diverse community can also enhance multicultural education if representatives from the various ethnic groups are chosen and the decision-making power is held jointly and equally by all members of the board. When each part of the educational institution addresses the issues of multicultural education and institutional racism, multicultural classroom materials will become fully effective.

I have chosen to address the issue of institutional racism through a book on multicultural curriculum development because I believe that "through guided classroom interaction, students' interracial attitudes may become more positive and accepting" (Chesler, 1971, p. 613). I have directed the book to teachers because they are the critical link between institutional racism and multicultural education. Teachers guide the interaction that Chesler describes. Each teacher will choose, from a range of levels, the extent of her or his involvement in multicultural education. No matter what level of involvement the teacher chooses, she or he will be guiding students' interactions toward an acceptance of racial, ethnic, and cultural diversity. Teachers who are very involved will design the entire classroom environment to reflect multiculturalism.

Teachers' own racial attitudes are a crucial ingredient in determining the success of multicultural education. Research has shown that there is a strong positive relationship between a child's perceptions of the teacher's feelings about her or him and the child's perception of her or his own value (Davidson & Lang, 1960). Because teachers' attitudes do affect their work with children, it is necessary for them to examine their own racial attitudes. All of us who have grown up in the United States have experienced the racist and sexist attitudes that exist in our society. Each of us has incorporated those attitudes into our own personal value systems to some degree, however unintentionally. Unless teachers understand the complexities and the deadly, pervasive nature of institutional racism, true multicultural education cannot take place.

# Understanding Child
# Development _____ 2

Young children are necessarily concerned with finding out who
they are and what they can do. As they develop, children move out
from themselves and away from their total involvement with their
own growth. They grow toward an acceptance of their role in a
society of individuals who work for other people's growth and
well-being as well as for their own. Facilitating a child's process of
moving from self-involvement to caring about and taking responsibility for others is part of a teacher's job. One way of facilitating the
process is by adopting a multicultural approach when designing a
learning environment for young children.

The child development framework presented in this book reflects
a combination of two philosophies: the developmental-interaction
point of view (Biber, 1977; Biber, Shapiro, & Wickens, 1971; Shapiro & Biber, 1972), and a philosophy of education for human relations (Taba, 1955). Essential to both philosophies is the goal of
helping children grow into caring adults involved with the people
and material objects that compose their environment.

Biber et al. (1971) describe the developmental-interaction theory
as follows:

> *Developmental* refers to the emphasis on identifiable patterns of
> growth and modes of experiencing and responding associated
> with increasing chronological age. *Interaction* refers to the em-
> phasis on the individual's interaction with the environment. It
> indicates the central importance of the child's interaction with

other people, adults and children, as well as with material objects of the environment; it refers also to the interaction between cognitive and affective spheres of development. It is a formulation which places comparable stress on the nature of the environment and on the patterns of the responding child, assuming an environment which provides maximum opportunity for engagement. (p. 6)

Taba's philosophy of education emphasizes the importance of counteracting influences that "cultivate" children's ethnocentricity. Taba alerts teachers to the necessity of developing in students an awareness of the positive aspects of cultural diversity.

The development of a cosmopolitan sensitivity and of a capacity to respond to human problems, values and feelings is a central task in education for human relations. Each individual grows up in a somewhat limiting cultural shell by virtue of the fact that the immediate primary groups in which a growing person is socialized are culturally unique. While living in today's world requires a broad orientation to life, some American communities are still bounded by qualifications regarding race, economic status, and ethnic origin. These differences tend to be maintained by separation of residence areas, by separate patterns of social association, and, therefore, by different life experiences. These experiences in the hemmed in cultural climates tend to cultivate ethnocentricity, or a tendency to interpret all other persons' behavior, values, and motivations in terms of one's own values. (p. 100)

In keeping with these two philosophies, this chapter explores three topics at length: first, the development of preschool children; next, how learning styles and ethnicity affect behavior; and finally, how racial awareness and racial attitudes develop.

## THE PRESCHOOL CHILD

Within the time identified as the preschool years, a great many exciting changes take place in the child. Between the ages of two-and-a-half and five, children change vastly in terms of their relationships with other people, their patterns of play, and their approaches to problem solving. "The preschool years are a time of rapid fluctuations, between overdependence and eager independence, between competence and ineptitude, between maturity and infantilism . . . between winsome affection and sudden antisocial destructiveness" (Stone & Church, 1973, pp. 262–63). While young preschool children are like toddlers in many ways, older preschool children—five-year-olds—are articulate, skilled, and have a strong sense of self. The preschool teacher who is knowledgeable about the changes that occur in the intervening years is able to create developmentally appropriate curricula for each child.

## Relationships with Other People

Very young children relate primarily to members of their immediate families. People outside the family seem to be of little importance to the infant and toddler. During the preschool years, the focus of attention begins to shift. The child's circle of significant people grows wider. If a preschool-age child is in a nursery school or day-care center, she or he necessarily comes in contact with at least one additional important adult, the teacher. The child also becomes part of a larger group of peers. Gradually the child grows comfortable with the new group of people, although the adjustment may be a difficult one.

The preschool child is cognitively and affectively egocentric. Egocentrism, identified as characteristic of the young child's thinking by Swiss psychologist Jean Piaget, is often confused with selfishness. Egocentrism in young children refers not to doing something for one's own benefit but rather to the child's total inability to see another point of view. Egocentric thought may cause children to act in ways that adults interpret as selfish behavior. However, according to Piaget, before the age of six or seven children are cognitively and socially incapable of acting in any other way (Ginsburg & Opper, 1979). Clearly, then, one cannot expect a young child to be able to transcend her- or himself in order to see that she or he is only one of many children in a classroom. Actions that may seem selfish or self-centered are simply the child's acting out of her or his view of the world. Therefore one of the crucial jobs for an adult involved with young children is helping the child learn to be concerned for and to value other people. The development of sympathy and empathy are relevant at this point. The child, as she or he grows less centered on her- or himself, begins to sympathize with her or his peers. In situations in which they themselves are not threatened, toddlers are capable of showing sympathetic behavior toward their immediate families, but it is not until the preschool years that the child can even begin to be genuinely concerned for and sympathetic to others' needs (Stone & Church, 1973).

Egocentrism is a necessary stage of development for young children, and, as Stone and Church have noted, "egocentrism provides the foundation for *ethnocentrism*, taking for granted the ways of behaving, the value and the ideas of the people among whom one grows up" (p. 90). It is interesting to note that while children outgrow their egocentrism, their ethnocentrism remains. One explanation for this phenomenon is that egocentrism is not a quality supported by middle-class American culture. There are all sorts of maxims encouraging children to be less egocentric. The Golden Rule—"Do unto others as you would have them do unto you"—for example, and the saying "Share and share alike" warn children that they must give up their childish, selfish ways. Ethnocentrism, however, is firmly rooted in our culture. We expect everyone to speak English and to adhere to our culture's rules. We assume, as a culture, that everyone shares our values and, if not, that they should. The importance of multicultural education for preschool children, then, becomes clear. With positive early experiences in multicultural education, children can be helped to move from egocentrism to an understanding and appreciation of ethnic diversity rather than being bound by an ethnocentric perspective.

## Patterns of Play

Play is part of every child's growth process. For the preschool child, play is the vehicle through which an enormous amount of learning takes place. Preschool children use play to practice skills they have learned. For example, a child may make a game of walking upstairs backwards. Children also use play to explore unknown situations. Jerome Bruner (1976) stresses that through play children are given "an excellent opportunity to try combinations of behaviour that would, under functional pressure, never be tried" (p. 38). The provision of a pressure-free, psychologically safe environment for preschoolers in which they can practice new roles and solutions without the threat of consequences that may occur in nonplay situations supports the children's growth and learning.

Dramatic play is a critical activity for preschool children. Through dramatic play a child is able to try on new roles or solve problems in a variety of ways. For example, a child's dramatic play may involve assuming the role of the powerful parent who must discipline a disobedient child. In addition, through the medium of dramatic play a child can experience another child's view of the world. The child also experiences the positive effects of cooperating with other children in dramatic play without risking her or his own egocentric world view. Thus teachers who plan their classroom activities to support both spontaneous play and a variety of social interactions help children learn to coordinate their own needs with the needs of others. In general, play can enable children to grow out of their egocentric and ethnocentric picture of the world.

## Problem Solving

Preschool children tend to take things at face value and are inclined to believe what they see. They are not yet able to imagine alternative solutions to situations or problems. This is another aspect of a young child's egocentricity and is true in both the cognitive and affective spheres of development. For example, in the cognitive domain young children are not able to reverse operations (Ginsburg & Opper, 1979). That is, they are not able to retrace their steps. Thus, when a three-year-old block builder is told it is time to clean up, she or he will either remove the first block used, which is, of course, at the bottom, or knock the whole building down instead of unbuilding the structure from the top down. The young builder is not able to see the alternative solution of disassembling the building by first removing the last block used.

Young children also do what Piaget has labeled "transductive thinking." That is, the child moves from one specific piece of information to another without forming generalizations (Ginsburg & Opper). Further, the young child is able to concentrate on only one attribute of an object at a time. Thus the preschool child is unable to get an overall view of the world. Toward the end of the preschool years the child begins organized language and thought processes

and is able to transcend her- or himself and the here and now. As thought processes grow more complex, problem-solving skills become more logical.

Similarly, in the affective domain, if two young children want the same toy the only solution either of them can imagine is totally egocentric. Each child believes she or he should have the toy. Again, adults play an important role in offering various solutions to the children. In this situation the teacher might find an additional, similar toy or ask the children to take turns, being careful to monitor the sharing so that one child does not benefit at the other's expense.

Further, the preschool child is not always able to differentiate between what is fantasy and what is reality. For example, the people on television seem as real to the child as the people in a store; dreams are as real as events that occur when she or he is awake. Many commonplace activities seem like magic to preschool children; electric lights come on mysteriously, just as cars are run by unseen powers. The story of the princess kissing a toad and turning it into a prince is no more astounding than elevators that go up and down simply at the push of a button. As children get older, they become increasingly concerned with determining what is truth, reality, and fact. For preschool children adults play a vital role as reality agents. Children rely on adults to bring them back into the real world should their fantasies take them too far afield—as they do, for example, when children have nightmares.

Part of preschool children's charm lies in their constant change and growth. During these years they grow from being very egocentric to being caring and sympathetic toward other people. Their inability to differentiate between fantasy and reality enables them to enjoy the world of make-believe and at the same time keeps them very vulnerable. Although the unrefined nature of their problem-solving skills is frequently frustrating both to them and to adults with whom they share their lives, the children's excitement at exploring new knowledge and skills eases the frustrations. In essence, rapid shifts in temperament and behavior, fluctuation between growing, logical thinking and misconceptions, and continually varying responses to environment characterize the preschool child.

## LEARNING STYLES

### Learning Styles and Ethnicity

Each of us has our individual learning style. We approach problems differently; we ask different questions, and we ask questions differently. Some of us prefer to learn by listening to information being discussed. Others seek information from books. Still others must immerse themselves in an experience by observing or attempting the actual thing to be learned. That children are also individuals with personal styles of learning is a frequently ignored aspect of teaching.

Learning styles can be categorized as visual (reading), aural (listening), or physical (doing things) (Clark, 1967). This does not mean that a child who appears to learn best by speaking and listening cannot also benefit from physical or "hands-on" experiences. It does mean, according to Clark, that opportunities to learn that take advantage of a child's preferred learning style are apt to yield the most permanent learning. In short, we all have different ways of internalizing our experiences, our own best way to learn. By helping students discover their own particular style of learning, we can help them learn more efficiently and effectively.

There is some evidence that learning styles are partially determined by ethnicity and culture (Cole, 1971). For purposes of this book, *culture* will be defined as a people's way of doing things. This refers to all of the value and belief systems, ways of thinking, acting, and responding. In an article on learning and ethnicity, Wilma Longstreet (1978) defines *ethnicity* as "that part of cultural development which occurs prior to the onset of a child's abstract intellectual powers as a result of his direct, personal contacts with the people around him and with his immediate environment" (p. 63). Thus if the teacher is to enhance children's use of their preferred learning styles, she or he needs to be aware of and knowledgeable about the children's cultural and ethnic backgrounds.

There is, indeed, a fine line between awareness of the potential effects of ethnicity on learning styles and expecting a child of a particular ethnic group to behave in a particular way. Ideally, the teacher does not view any child as a cultural or ethnic representative but responds to each one as an individual for whom culture or ethnicity is merely one aspect of her or his personality. The key to making this distinction is observation, for observation is one of the teacher's most important ways of learning about a child. The teacher tries to observe each child without expectations based on race, ethnicity, sex, or life experience and uses the information gained through observation to design appropriate learning experiences for the child.

Learning to observe children objectively is a difficult process. A critical ingredient in objective observation is an awareness of the suppositions one brings to the observational process. Just as the examination of one's racial attitudes is essential prior to setting up a multicultural classroom environment, so an exploration of the assumptions and expectations fostered by one's ethnic heritage is important before beginning to observe children. For instance, if a teacher comes from a culture that values learning by example she or he might find it difficult to objectively observe a child who learns by actively exploring learning materials; the teacher might unconsciously feel that the child was simply making a mess. If the teacher were aware of his or her own biases, objective observation would be easier. (For more information about observation in general, see

Almy and Genishi's *Ways of Studying Children* [1979] and Cohen and Stern's *Observing and Recording the Behavior of Young Children* [1983].) The object is not to ignore ethnicity but to seek to heighten one's sensitivity to what is valued and taught in particular cultures, rather than relying on generalizations about a culture or race.

In some Hispanic or Spanish-speaking cultures children are taught that making eye contact with an adult is disrespectful. Being reprimanded for looking away when talking with a teacher may therefore be very confusing for an Hispanic child. Further, because many teachers value eye contact and relate it to the ability to interact well with people, the refusal to make eye contact may be viewed as a behavior to be corrected. If a teacher is aware of this part of a child's cultural training, however, it is unlikely that she or he would require a child to do something so contrary to what the child has already learned.

The ways in which new information is processed differ from culture to culture. Some children are taught new skills and information by observing an activity closely for a long period of time. For example, Vera John (1972) suggests that Navajo children have highly developed visual discrimination and fine motor skills and learn to absorb the world through sight and touch. They learn best by observing an activity for a long time before trying to do it themselves. For some Navajo children, then, teaching strategies that emphasize demonstration and materials that invite active manipulation may be most appropriate to the child's already developed learning strategy. A teacher's verbal direction to "match the blocks of the same color" may not be as successful as a demonstration of matching by the teacher or a classmate.

The child's perception of time is also relevant to learning styles (Hovey, 1975). Different cultural groups experience time in different ways. For example, being "on time" in some cultures means getting to an appointment when all of the things that needed to be done before that appointment have been completed. Instead of time's being measured by discrete hour and minute segments, it is measured by the length of time that it takes to complete a task. Werner, Bierman, and French (1971) suggest that for this reason some children do poorly on performance tests that are based on white, middle-class understanding of time as minutes and hours. Pacing activities on an individual basis and giving advance notice of transition times, so that a child will have time to reorient her or his internal time mechanism, are two ways to respect a child's different perception of time.

Some Asian-American children are taught to value silence and to avoid overt displays of emotion (Kuroiwa, 1975). For some teachers who are more comfortable with the white American, middle-class manner of spontaneous, verbal expression of emotion, the Asian-American child may seem shy and withdrawn. In order to support the child's preference for not expressing emotion openly, the teacher will want to provide a variety of avenues for the expression of feelings. Mime, charades, creative movement, and dramatic play can all serve as vehicles through which a child can learn to communicate.

In short, learning styles can be affected by culture and ethnicity. The examples of behavior cited here are illustrative, rather than comprehensive or conclusive. Teachers who wish to understand the learning styles of children in multiethnic classes can frequently get useful clues by learning about the cultures of the children in their classes. Some sources for particular cultures are cited in appendix B, "Bibliography on Institutional Racism," but culture and ethnicity are not the sole determinants of learning style. It is essential that teachers not make assumptions about a child's learning style solely on the basis of the child's cultural heritage. Not all Asian-American children learn to refrain from verbal expression of emotion; not all Navajo children learn most readily through demonstration; and not all Hispanic children look away when speaking with adults. These examples are given simply to show possibilities through which learning can take place within a framework of respect for cultural and ethnic diversity. The responsibility of the teacher is to determine the preferred learning style for each child in the classroom and to plan that child's school experience accordingly.

## Identifying Learning Styles

The first step in identifying a child's learning style is to observe the child's various ways of interacting in a learning environment. The goal is to determine as accurately as possible what pattern of work habits a child uses in her or his most successful learning encounters. Information from experiences that are frustrating to a

child can also be useful. For example, if a child seems to be unable
to engage in productive activity after verbal directions have been
given the teacher can look to see if there is a pattern of inability to
respond to learning situations that emphasize listening. If so, the
teacher can then try using pictorial or written directions, demon-
strating a particular procedure for the child, or encouraging the
child to observe other children engaged in the desired activity.

Once a pattern is identified, the teacher can attempt to determine
how much of a child's learning style may be connected with her or
his culture and how much is due to the child's individual personality. Longstreet (1978) has outlined a format for considering cultural
influences on learning style that is useful for teachers who are
attempting to make changes in their classroom activities to address
differences in learning style. Longstreet considers both the factors
that affect a child's predisposition to learn and the behavioral patterns that affect how learning takes place.

According to Longstreet, there are three factors that influence a
child's predisposition to learning: classroom atmosphere, relevance
of information, and appropriateness of materials (pp. 67–68). The
atmosphere in which learning best takes place differs from one child
to another. Riessman (1966) suggests that we too often expect learning to take place only in a particularly quiet atmosphere: "Strangely
enough, some people do their best studying in a noisy place, or
with certain sounds such as music or even traffic in the background" (p. 16). If a child has a large family and is accustomed to a
lot of noise, an exceedingly quiet classroom could require a difficult
adjustment. If, on the other hand, the child's home environment is
very quiet, the child may have difficulty concentrating while other
children are moving about or talking to one another.

Obviously, then, cultural traits are not the only variables to be
taken into account when assessing the kind of learning environment
a child needs. It is important as well to consider messages the child
has received early in life about noise, neatness, and discipline when
working. In order to accommodate to the various needs of the
children, teachers can provide different types of learning environments within the classroom. There should be quiet places in the
room for children whose tolerance of noise is low and more open
spaces for children who work well with more stimuli. For children
who seem to need a working space that is always theirs, specific

desks or table spaces could be set aside. The children for whom a specific space does not appear to be necessary can work in various parts of the room as their tasks demand.

The relevance of the material in a curriculum to the child's concerns partially determines how children respond to the presentation of material. Because of their egocentrism, young children are most comfortable with content areas that are somewhat familiar to them. They attend better to topics that have some connection to their own experience. For example, reading stories that have as the main characters white families in a suburban or rural setting is simply not relevant to black, brown, or white children in an urban, integrated school. These children cannot be expected to be excited about catching fish in a stream when they have never even seen a stream. Hence it is crucial that the learning environment include not only materials with which a child is familiar but also a variety of cultural and ethnic materials, regardless of the racial composition of the class. Only in this way can children's own experiences and sense of culture be supported while they are being introduced to other ethnic groups.

Finally, the appropriateness of curriculum materials, curriculum content, and classroom practices are also instrumental in determining a child's predisposition to learning. For example, if discussions concerning sex, death, or divorce are not appropriate topics in a young child's ethnic group or family unit, the child may be very reluctant to participate in a discussion of such matters in class. In this case a strategy based on the teacher's knowledge of the individual child is more appropriate. Sometimes children find it easier and more acceptable to deal with the concept indirectly. For example, it may be less threatening for some children to talk about the death of an animal than the death of a person. Often young children's questions about death and divorce are really questions about "What can I control?" The teacher can design a curriculum that will help children understand what things they can control and what things they cannot. For example, we can control the way we move our bodies, but not how tall we grow. We can control our behavior, but we often cannot control our feelings.

Similarly, if a child has learned at home that it is important to keep her or his clothes clean at school that child may have difficulty participating fully in painting a large and messy mural. The provision of a smock or play clothes for this child may allow her or him to participate more fully and freely in the messy project. Teachers should be aware of how appropriate their requests or directions are and be prepared to offer children alternatives that will make them more comfortable.

Thus the teacher plays a critical role in influencing a child's predisposition to learn by providing children with an atmosphere that includes a variety of learning opportunities, by presenting information that is relevant to their environment and culture, and by adapting the curriculum to make it appropriate to individual family concerns.

In addition to describing these factors that influence a child's predisposition to learn, Longstreet describes six behavioral patterns that affect how learning takes place and that she feels might be influenced by culture: (1) the child's manner of participating in activities; (2) the attention she or he gives to activities; (3) the ways in which she or he processes information; (4) the manner in which the child presents her or his thoughts to others; (5) the ways in which she or he asks questions; and (6) the kinds of questions the child asks (pp. 68–70). Again, by carefully observing children in a classroom a teacher can find patterns that demonstrate how a child's learning style affects her or his participation in the group. Jotting down daily or weekly notes on what is observed can help the teacher to discover patterns of interaction with peers and materials.

In order to accommodate the various learning styles of the children in a classroom, teachers have two responsibilities. First, by providing flexible classroom environments teachers encourage all children to learn regardless of their individual learning styles. By being sensitive to children's learning styles and by being aware of the cultural influences on those learning styles, teachers offer each child the opportunity to grow and learn in ways most suitable to her or him. Further, in a classroom in which many learning styles are encouraged, more models for styles of problem solving and decision making are available for children to choose from should their own not be successful. Second, teachers need to be aware of their own learning styles, which have been determined by their own ethnicity, life experiences, and personality. They can find out about their learning styles by examining the same behavioral patterns in themselves that they would examine in a child to identify

her or his learning style. Through this awareness teachers will be better able to recognize their own tendencies toward ethnocentrism and will be more apt to adapt their teaching style to fit the learning styles of the children.

## THE DEVELOPMENT OF RACIAL AWARENESS AND RACIAL ATTITUDES

Children are frequently represented as being "color-blind," that is, unaware of what color or race people are. A British minister of education, for example, was quoted as saying, "Young children seem to be quite unconscious of colour differences, and there is no more pleasing sight than to watch in some of our primary schools groups of children of different racial origins working and playing together" (Pushkin & Veness, 1974, p. 23). This same sense of children as oblivious to differences in color or culture is prevalent in our country as well (Beuf, 1977). However, this perception is directly contradicted by the facts. Young children are very aware of race and color differences. They ask frequent questions, most often related to their own physical characteristics and those of others, about matters such as skin color and hair color (Derman-Sparks, Higa, & Sparks, 1980).

There is general agreement among researchers that the development of children's racial awareness has begun by age three or four. By that time children seem to recognize which people have black skin and which have white skin (Katz, 1976). (Far less research has been done using people of color other than black people. We will assume, however, that racial awareness in yellow, red, and brown children occurs at the same age that it does in black and white children.) Some theorists (for example, Goodman, 1964) believe that this recognition is part of young children's process of establishing their identity; children determine what they are and what they are not.

Positive and negative feelings about race seem to appear at about the same age as awareness of race. In Goodman's classic study of 103 black and white children (1952), which pinpointed the age of racial awareness at three to four years, 25 percent of the children also exhibited some negative feelings about black people; one white child, for example, talked about wanting to cut a black man's head off with an axe. In a study done in the Northeast with three- to five-year-old children (Porter, 1971), white children were more positive about their skin color than black children were about theirs. The white children applied positive adjectives to their color; black children applied less positive adjectives to their skin color. In a study done by Southern California day-care workers recording young children's comments about race (Derman-Sparks et al., 1980), a frequently reported question from black children was "Why do I have to be black?" Thus it is clear that young children already have positive and negative feelings about race.

Although there is much evidence to show that the foundations of negative racial attitudes are laid sometime during the preschool years (Williams & Morland, 1976), how these attitudes are developed is a question that has intrigued many researchers. Some have focused on parents' racial attitudes as determinants of children's attitudes. Morris (1981) reported, for example, that teachers in her study held parents responsible for their children's negative racial attitudes. Although there is no substantive data to support this hypothesis, this theory is still widely held.

Other researchers believe that children's negative racial attitudes are reinforced by the culture in general, by media, by adults, and by other children in the child's life. Citron (1971) states that children's attitudes are shaped by the segregated nature of society; white children are under the illusion that they are the only children in the world, and children of color see themselves as different from and less worthy than the rest. Stabler and Jordan (1971) and Porter (1971) argue that children's negative racial attitudes are due in part to their internalization of the positive associations of the word *white* and the negative associations of the word *black* in the English language. Still another researcher (P.A. Katz, 1976) believes that negative attitudes are caused by the combination of these factors rather than any single one. In her exhaustive review of recent research concerning racial attitudes, Katz suggests that more research is needed to determine the cognitive, perceptual, and reinforcement elements of attitude acquisition and the interaction among these elements. At this stage of research we are currently unable to say with certainty what factors are involved in the development of negative racial attitudes.

This uncertainty concerning the causes of negative racial attitudes makes the job of the teacher all the more difficult. If it were established, for example, that children learned their racial attitudes from their parents, then energy could be focused on working with parents. However, failure to isolate one element responsible for developing racial attitudes does not imply that nothing can be done. For, as Morris states, "Direct experiences, observations and internalization of concepts inherent in the environment are powerful determinants of children's attitudes and behaviors" (1981, p. 236). Thus teachers who are trying to combat the development of negative racial attitudes in children will work to create an environment in which children develop a sense of themselves and of those from different cultural backgrounds as vital, worthwhile people, each with special uniqueness and value.

# Presenting
# Multicultural Education
## to Parents —————————————— 3

**W**orking with the parents of the children in a class is an integral part of the teacher's job. This task has many aspects, one of which is interpreting the curriculum to parents. Because multicultural education brings to adults' minds the sensitive and emotion-laden topic of race, it is important that teachers both communicate the goals and purposes of this approach directly with parents and be willing to deal with the parents' thoughts and feelings about race. Understanding the complexities of their own racial attitudes helps teachers to be open and direct with parents about the curriculum and less judgmental about parents' responses. Thus an effective presentation of multicultural education to parents requires that teachers first examine their own racial attitudes and values. In other words, teachers cannot raise parents' awareness about injustice and inequalities if they have not assessed their own attitudes in this area.

## EXAMINING OUR RACIAL ATTITUDES

The examination of our own attitudes is not a simple task. It is a long, difficult process for all people, because racial attitudes are so deeply ingrained. It is important to keep in mind that the goal of exploring racial attitudes is not necessarily immediate attitude change but rather awareness of attitudes. It is unrealistic to expect racial attitudes to change quickly.

The exploration of attitudes about race begins with an examination of some basic definitions. Although prejudice, discrimination, and racism are all part of the same problem, they are not the same entities, and each manifests itself in different ways in our society. *Prejudice* is defined as "an unfavorable opinion formed beforehand or without knowledge" and as "hatred or dislike directed against a racial, religious, or national group" (*Random House Dictionary*, 1978). Prejudice is an interpersonal attitude: Johnny does not like Yolanda because she is Puerto Rican; Yolanda does not like Johnny because he is white. Ms. Jones does not like Ms. Smith because Ms. Smith is black; Ms. Smith does not like Ms. Jones because Ms. Jones is white. No real action is taken on anybody's part, but there are a lot of unpleasant feelings. Prejudice is a personal matter between individuals or between an individual and a group of people.

Discrimination has its basis in prejudice, but the consequences are more serious than those of prejudice. Ms. Allen is not promoted from assistant principal to principal because she is black; Ms. Boynton disciplines her pupil Jake more severely because he is black. Mr. Katz is not elected to the school board because he is black. In each case these people are discriminated against on the basis of their color. They are not treated as they would have been had they been white. People of color can also discriminate against white people. A working definition of *discrimination* is "a distinction in favor of or against a person or thing on the basis of prejudice" (*Random House Dictionary*, 1978).

The implications of racism are more far-reaching than those of either prejudice or discrimination. *Racism* is defined as "any attitude, action, or institutional structure which subordinates a person or group because of his or their color" (U.S. Commission on Civil Rights, 1970). The key to this definition is subordination. Individuals or groups of people are kept in subordinate, less powerful, less important positions on the basis of their color. When a person subordinates people of color on the basis of racial prejudice, that prejudice becomes individual racism. For example, a teacher who has lower expectations of children of color than she or he has of white children in the classroom is exhibiting individual racism.

Institutional structures that subordinate a person or group because of color are the most pernicious and pervasive form of racism. Institutional racism is so embedded in our society's institutional structure that white individuals no longer feel personally responsible for its perpetuation. An example of institutional racism in the area of education is the continued use of culturally biased IQ tests, such as the Wechsler Intelligence Scale for Children—Revised (WISC-R), that "elevate the mean score for Anglo children . . . and . . . define groups that differ systematically in their language, values, or behavioral style from the majority group as abnormal" (Mercer, 1979, p. 20). Another manifestation of institutional racism is cultural racism. Cultural racism outlives any single individual and pervades the thinking, speech, and actions of whole groups of people. In the English language, for example, many of our definitions and uses for the words *white* and *black* reinforce notions of white superiority and black inferiority (Burgest, 1973). From the ethnocentricity revealed in the term *flesh-colored* crayon to the casual racial stereotyping in expressions like "sitting Indian style" and "Chinese fire drill," the biases in everyday English reflect a deeply ingrained cultural racism.

In our educational system, as in every other institution in contemporary society, institutional racism is prevalent. A brief look at the areas of curriculum, ability grouping, and school administration illustrates some of the ways in which institutional racism manifests itself. Curriculum materials are, perhaps, the most obvious of all examples. Although some improvements have been made in this area, materials still contain stereotyped representations of people of nonwhite races. Books, records, pictures, and other audiovisual materials continue to inform children that all Indians live in tepees, that all Eskimos live in igloos, that all Chinese people operate laundries (Grant & Grant, 1981).

Another example of institutional racism in schools is seen in curriculum priorities. Because a curriculum reflects the system of values and priorities of those who devise it (Chesler, 1967), it is important to look at what is put into the curriculum and what is omitted. For example, in an attempt to address the issue of cultural awareness, some designers of curricula include a week to study black people, a week to study Native Americans, and a week to study Mexican-Americans, without integrating a multicultural approach into the rest of the year's program. Although the "black heritage week" approach seems to be an improvement on the old ways, fifty-one "white weeks" remain in the calendar year in which children continue to be taught in an ethnocentric manner.

Ability grouping, or the tracking system, is another way in which children of color suffer discrimination and institutional racism is maintained. When children are tracked, white middle-class children in the upper tracks frequently come to feel that red, black, yellow, and brown children in the lower tracks are inferior. These children in the lower groups feel bad about themselves because of their position within the tracking system. Black, brown, red, and yellow children in the upper groups think that being a person of color is not as good as being white or there would be more children like them in the higher groups. Finally, children often remain in the ability group they are placed in at the beginning of their schooling, and frequently they achieve only to that level of expectation, regardless of their intelligence (Holt, 1964).

A lack of role models for children of color reinforces the messages given by the tracking system. Despite an increased number of black, red, yellow, and brown people in positions of authority today, there is still a notable imbalance of power in the schools. The majority of principals in our educational institutions are white men (U.S. Equal Employment Opportunity Commission, 1977, 1978). In the absence of alternative/authority figures, children could assume that white men are the only people who can run things. Further, white girls and girls and boys of color might not even strive for decision-making jobs, because of the lack of role models available to them. At the same time that children see white men in positions of authority in schools, they see black, brown, red, and yellow adults in less important, more menial jobs, serving as teachers' aides, janitors, and cooks in the cafeterias. This institutionalized racial imbalance reinforces children's perceptions that this is the way it is supposed to be.

Teachers who are aware of the institutional racism inherent in the educational system will be better able to examine their own racial attitudes. One way to begin this process is to look at one's own experiences with issues of race, to note one's response when the experience occurred, and to look at the present-day response to such an experience. J. H. Katz (1978) suggests examining the fol-

lowing types of experiences as a beginning: (1) the experience of
first meeting a person of a different color, of realizing the similarities and differences in life experiences; (2) the experience of
discovering that school tests often misrepresent history or tell only
part of the story (for example, realizing that slaves were not content
on plantations in the South or discovering that thousands of
Japanese-Americans were interned in this country during World
War II, though the majority of German-Americans were not); (3)
the experience of realizing that people are treated differently according to their color; and (4) the experience of being the only
person of color in an all white group or the only white person
among people of color (pp. 106–7).

Some experiences involving race are more directly related to
teaching—for example, being a black teacher with a class composed
entirely of white children, or being a white, English-speaking
teacher with a class of Mexican-American children who speak
Spanish in the home. Each of these situations has its own ramifica-
tions, in terms of parents' responses to the teacher, which will be
addressed in the next section of this chapter. In terms of exploring
one's own racial attitudes, however, there are underlying commonalities in these experiences. One common factor is the sense of
being different from the children and parents with whom one
works and having a separate set of racial experiences that one brings
to the classroom situation. In these instances it is helpful to focus
not only on the racial attitudes about the group with whom one is
working but also on the feelings that go along with being the only
person in a group who does not share a common cultural heritage.

Another aspect of such a teaching experience that might be
explored is the motivation behind putting oneself in such a position.
Obviously there are some instances in which a teacher is assigned to
a school without regard for her or his preference. In other situations, however, teachers choose to work with classes composed entirely of children from a different racial group than their own. In
the case of the white teacher in the Spanish-speaking class, is the
motivation for such a choice wanting to "help" a group that is
perceived to be "disadvantaged"? Or in the case of the black teacher
in an all white class, is the motivation to prove that one's own racial
group is competent and not so different from white people? Clearly
there is a wide range of reasons that would motivate a teacher to

make such a choice—some emotional and others, perhaps, financial. It would be important, in terms of one's own awareness of the attitudes with which one enters a situation, to spend time identifying personal reasons for teaching in a class of culturally different children. In short, preparing to talk with parents about multicultural education provides teachers the opportunity, and frequently the impetus, to explore their own racial attitudes. The teacher's job is to use that opportunity to its fullest in order to better prepare her- or himself to work well with the parents and children in a teaching situation.

## TALKING WITH PARENTS ABOUT MULTICULTURAL EDUCATION

Interpreting the multicultural curriculum to parents is one of the teacher's most important responsibilities. Because none of us is free from prejudice, parents may be concerned about the multicultural approach, and teachers must be aware of this fact when dealing with parents. Racial attitudes are so complex and so deeply imbedded in people's psychological makeup that a great variety of responses from parents is possible. Reactions may range from the very positive to the highly negative.

One way to deal with such a situation is to anticipate the parents' responses and questions. This type of preparation should help a teacher to be less defensive when presenting multicultural education. For example, in a class composed primarily or exclusively of white children, the teacher might expect that some parents might not see any reason for a multicultural approach. In this case the teacher may want to emphasize that the children's exposure to and understanding of different cultures is excellent preparation for life in our society, which is multiracial and multicultural. It is certainly a necessary part of any teacher's job to support children's growth as social beings, and by definition a social being is one who lives successfully in a world composed of people who are like us and people who are different from us. A teacher in this situation might emphasize that failing to provide a variety of experiences would be leaving children ill equipped to function in the world.

In a traditional educational system some parents may view a

multicultural approach to their children's education as different from the education they themselves obtained and thus may feel it to be inappropriate. These parents may even be suspicious of such an approach. If this is the case, one can stress the fact that through such a curriculum each child's self-concept is nurtured. Because the approach to multicultural education affirms individual differences, each child will know that she or he is special and valued. When describing the curriculum to these parents, the multicultural approach can be treated as only one aspect of the curriculum—a basic one, to be sure, but only one aspect. Rather than suggesting that a multicultural curriculum is unusual or experimental, the teacher can present it as the way curricula should be.

The most important strategy for presenting multicultural education to parents involves listening to their fears and prejudices in an accepting and nonjudgmental manner. Making parents defensive and angry will not win their support for the curriculum. One can ask the parents to talk about their fears or hesitancy regarding the curriculum. Again, all of us, regardless of color, have unresolved feelings about racial issues. By simply listening to a parent's concerns in a nonjudgmental manner, a teacher allows the parent an opportunity to examine her or his own feelings and fears. Frequently this process of examination diffuses the parents' negative reactions. To conclude this conversation, the teacher may explain that the multicultural approach is the one that she or he feels is most appropriate for the healthy development of all children.

White teachers are frequently surprised at the hesitancy with which black or Hispanic or Asian or Native American parents approach them. Teachers usually see themselves as caring, unprejudiced people who welcome the children and parents, regardless of color, into the classroom. A white teacher needs to remember that as a group white people have not treated people of color well. This is not to say that white teachers need to be bound to this history by guilt. Rather, it is important to know the actions of whites in the past and then to examine one's own actions today to determine that the teacher is doing all she or he can to work against the continuation of racial exploitation. It is also important to be aware that while the white teacher, as one individual, may not feel that she or he has oppressed people of color, parents may not trust the teacher, because she or he is white. White parents, too, are sometimes hesitant about teachers who are people of color. We live in such a segregated culture that white people frequently have little personal interaction with nonwhite people, particularly people of color in professional positions. Again, both patience and understanding of the parents' reservations are important. It is essential that all teachers be aware of the cultural history that parents bring to situations so that they do not have unrealistic expectations of establishing instant rapport and trust with them.

Another potentially problematic situation is a class that is mixed both racially and attitudinally. Here it is often helpful to bring parents together in an informal social situation, such as a class breakfast or an evening get-together, rather than the more formal school meeting. The teacher thus sets up a less threatening way for parents to meet and talk with each other about what they usually care most about: their children. However, there are several areas that need careful attention when organizing this kind of social function for families: work schedules of parents, other demands on parents' time, parents' fear of being in a strange, unknown situation, and lack of money to purchase food for the function. The problems of food can be readily solved if the teacher and children can do the cooking together, with parents' help should that be available. There is usually some money in the school budget for such functions.

A teacher's success in dealing with parents in any type of class depends on sensitivity to family needs and experience and basic respect for parents' ideas and values. The need for sensitivity and respect increases when dealing with the deeply personal issue of race. It is essential that communication lines between parents and teacher be strong and be always open. Regardless of points of view, if the parents and the teacher stop talking to each other, the real loser is the child.

# Preparing for
# Multicultural Education
# in the Classroom ——————4

$B$efore examining the specific ways in which teachers can develop a multicultural perspective in their classrooms (the subject of chapters 5 and 6), it is important to examine briefly the theoretical basis for such an effort. As part of that theoretical foundation, this chapter will provide some basic guidelines for dealing with the issue of race in the classroom and will cover the various possible levels of involvement at which a teacher can work toward creating a multicultural learning environment.

## THEORETICAL BASIS
## FOR A MULTICULTURAL PERSPECTIVE

One of the goals of any preschool curriculum is to help the young child move from her or his sheltered family unit into a much more complex environment. Taba (1962) states that "the curriculum should develop the knowledge and perspective which is commensurate with the kind of world in which we live, a world that . . . is composed of an unlimited variety of outlooks, backgrounds, and standards of living" (p. 213). Indeed, preschool is the beginning step in socializing the child, in helping the child change from an egocentric, ethnocentric person to one who understands and is sympathetic to people of considerable diversity.

Multicultural education is not something that can be grafted onto the preschool curriculum. Working with children toward the development of positive racial attitudes and the affirmation of differences is central to the philosophy underlying all that goes on in a classroom, regardless of the degree to which a teacher involves her- or himself in multicultural education. Education that is multicultural is built on nurturing a positive self-concept for all children from the earliest years. These strong, positive feelings about themselves should prepare children to be less threatened by change and by diversity. Multiculturalism is not solely concerned with developing good feelings of self in the children of color who are so frequently the victims of racism in the United States. Equally important is the positive depiction for white children of culturally different life experiences. Thus a classroom that reflects a multicultural perspective is a basic, supportive environment in which children of all races can grow and learn. Integral to this basic program is a commitment to broadening children's awareness of and natural acceptance of diverse cultural heritages.

There are obviously some ways in which the racial or ethnic composition of a classroom affects the techniques a teacher chooses to use in exposing young children to different cultures. There are not, however, as many differences as one might think. The primary difference is that in a heterogeneous classroom one is able to draw on the experiences of the children rather than to have to rely solely on pictures and books. For example, if there are Spanish-speaking children in a primarily English-speaking classroom, the children who speak English can learn Spanish words and phrases from the Spanish-speaking children and vice versa. Children love to know more than one name for an object or different ways to say "Good morning." Teachers in a heterogenous classroom have the luxury of being able to choose foods or games that come directly out of the class community. Teachers in a homogenous classroom, on the other hand, must provide a hypothetical multicultural community for their students. Even in a biracial classroom, however, it is important for children to see that there are other people of color in the world besides those represented in their class.

With encouragement to explore, to initiate activities, and to make the environment work for them, children are active participants in their own development and learning. In an environment rich in diversity, children are able to experience a variety of people, objects, and situations. However, because the young child is so egocentric developmentally, it would be inappropriate to barrage her or him with too much specific information about cultures and countries totally foreign to the child's own experience. Regardless of where the classroom is—in a large diverse urban community or in a homogeneous rural or surburban community—young children need to experience diversity without too many confusing specifics. For instance, by including pictures of Eskimo, Chinese, Asian, and African people on class bulletin boards, without talking directly about Alaska, China, Asia, or Africa as geographical and cultural entities, a teacher lets children know there are all kinds of people in the world. But at the same time this does not confuse children by giving them information too unrelated to their own situations. (It is important to note that although some pictures, such as pictures of American Indians in headdresses or Eskimos in igloos, can reinforce stereotypes, the ones used in the classroom can be carefully selected to avoid stereotypes.) By playing games or cooking foods or singing songs in ways that children from other cultures do, young children begin to see that people who do things differently are not frightening or wrong. Rather, learning new games or songs from children with other cultures makes life more interesting. By building on young children's own experiences, teachers can provide children with new experiences that expand their understanding, experiences that enable them to identify with and care about people of diverse backgrounds, values, and life-styles.

## GUIDELINES FOR DEALING WITH RACE IN THE CLASSROOM

A teacher can plan a curriculum that focuses on race and cultural differences, but even if she or he does not have such a plan, classroom conversations about racial issues often arise spontaneously. These can be difficult to anticipate and address. In some ways such conversations are the most critical, more important than planned discussions, because the impetus for them frequently springs directly from the children's concerns, from something they have noticed in the class or in the world around them. Young children, as has been mentioned, are aware of race and concerned about racial issues by the time they are four or five (Derman-Sparks, Higa, & Sparks, 1980; Goodman, 1952; Morris, 1981) and generally feel comfortable asking questions or expressing these concerns. To approach spontaneous conversations about race most effectively, it is helpful if the teacher has previously become comfortable with discussing such issues by considering what her or his personal responses might be. This is not an easy task for any adult in our contemporary society, but it will be difficult to encourage positive feelings about differences in the children if the teacher is ill at ease. (Some suggestions about how teachers can undertake this process were made in chapter 3.)

In addition, the teacher can plan to initiate discussions about race instead of avoiding them. He or she can deliberately find an occasion to talk about such things as skin color, hair, and the other physical characteristics that distinguish different races. One way to

do this is by introducing new materials. For example, one could read a new book about a Chinese family to the children and then talk about the appearance of the characters in the book. Cultural differences can also be explored. If a book or material contains racial stereotypes, the teacher should not ignore them but should find a place for them in the discussion. For example, after reading a book that portrays a traditional white nuclear family with mother at home and father at work, a conversation could begin with, "We know something that the person who wrote this book doesn't seem to know. Not all moms stay at home while daddies go to work," or "Not all of our families look like the one in this book." In this way the children's own life experiences and respect for differences can be validated and supported. Another way to initiate such discussions is by talking about the physical characteristics of the children themselves. This is particularly helpful in a classroom that is mixed racially, but it is possible to do it in a homogeneous classroom as well by talking about differences in hair color, eye color, and skin complexion.

The teacher who is comfortable with racial issues will respond to children's questions and racial concerns in a straightforward manner but without giving so much technical information that the children become confused. For example, in a racially diverse class a child may ask, "Why am I black and Jane is white? I want to be white so I can be like Jane." There are two concerns operating here: "Why do some people have one color of skin and some have another?" and "Why am I different?" Probably the most pressing concern for this young child lies in the second question, so a long discussion about skin pigmentation, melanin, and its role in determining skin color is unnecessary and inappropriate. More to the point would be a brief explanation: "Some people have more melanin in their skin than others, just as some people have black hair and some have red hair." Then one could address the second question by asking the child why she or he would like to be like Jane. At the root of the question may be a simple desire to be like a friend, or it may be the black child's feeling or observation that white children are better looking, or happier, or have more toys. If the child does seem to feel that being white is better, the teacher could help the child to discuss her or his perceptions about how skin color makes a difference in a person's life by asking such questions as "Do you like being _____ (the child's skin color or ethnic group)?" "Why or why not?" "Why would you want to be _____?" Through such discussions the child can begin to explore her or his ideas about skin color. These beginning conversations are important because they give the child, regardless of color, permission to talk about his or her confusing feelings about color of skin and race.

Racial slurs need to be dealt with directly when they arise. Suppose, for example, that a white child calls a black child "nigger." The first step in dealing with the situation is to ask the white child what she or he thinks the word means. After the child responds, the teacher can ask why he or she called the black child "nigger." Then the teacher might talk about the word, perhaps following Wilson's (1980a) suggestion: "If children want to know what the word means, they should be told the truth: 'It is a word that used to mean the color black. It came to be a word that means Black people. For a long time now it has been a word that means Black people are not as good as whites. It is a word that hurts' " (p. 18). The most important message the teacher can give children about all racial slurs is that it is not acceptable to use them—that they hurt people and perpetuate false ideas of cultural, ethnic, or racial inferiority.

Since it is not developmentally possible for young children to empathize with others' feelings, they cannot fully understand the power of racial slurs. It therefore does little good to say to young children, "How would you feel if someone called you a _____?" The best way to deal with racial slurs, after asking what provoked the name calling and then discussing what the word means, is simply to say, "In this classroom, calling people nigger (or 'honkie' or 'spic') is not okay. You may not do it." If the child then says, "But my father calls them 'niggers'," the teacher can say, "Yes, some people do, but in this classroom it is not all right." By handling the issue of the parent's racial attitudes in this way, the teacher lets the child know that some things are all right at home but not at school and vice versa, rather than asking the child to choose between parent and teacher.

Obviously, these guidelines address only the most fundamental issues. For an extended discussion of how to deal with the subject of race in the classroom, see the collection of articles entitled "Children, Race and Racism: How Race Awareness Develops" in Wilson (1980b).

# LEVELS OF INVOLVEMENT
# IN MULTICULTURAL EDUCATION

Because each teacher has different skills, teaching situations, and life experiences, it would be unrealistic to expect every teacher to bring the same talents or the same commitment to developing multicultural education for her or his students. While some teachers may be ready to redesign their entire program to reflect a multicultural society, others may want to begin with a less ambitious task.

There are six levels of involvement in multicultural education. Because the levels of involvement are cumulative, entry at a particular level assumes that the teacher has already incorporated the preceding levels into the class curriculum.

LEVEL 1: IMPLEMENTING A BASIC SOCIAL CURRICULUM

At this level the teacher is concerned with facilitating the development of children's fundamental social skills. Teachers who enter at this level would work toward the development of a strong self-concept and positive cultural identity in all children. This could be done by recognizing and celebrating a variety of holidays such as Hanukkah, Kwanza, and Christmas, as well as by personalizing children's lockers or cubbies and by displaying children's work. These teachers would also provide materials and experiences that require children to combine their energies to reach a common goal. One might use materials and activities that work only with two or more children, such as seesaws or walkie-talkies. Group projects such as making body tracings, murals, or class books might be planned to reinforce the idea that working together is fun and productive. Another objective for this level of involvement is to encourage children to practice taking another person's point of view. If children are given opportunities to work with people, such as babies or elderly adults, whose needs are unlike their own in some way, they can begin to experience concretely what it would be like to be someone with very different needs.

LEVEL 2: ENLARGING CHILDREN'S CULTURAL KNOWLEDGE BASE

At this level the teacher provides children with information about and understanding of other races, cultures, or ethnic groups, for example, by inviting parents to help children cook foods that are traditional in their cultures. Potato latkes, tabouleh, or rice and beans are examples of foods the parents might cook. Teachers might also invite community members to share special skills related to their cultural heritage with the children, such as weaving and storytelling. To introduce children to people working in culture-related settings, trips to ethnic grocery stores or stores that feature culture-specific goods would be appropriate. It is important when planning these trips to avoid reinforcing stereotypes like Chinese people working in laundries or Native Americans stringing beads in a reproduction of an Indian village.

Another objective of level 2 is to present materials that include and value a variety of cultural, racial, and ethnic experiences. This can be done by using books that include characters from different cultural groups and by providing baby dolls or people block accessories from various racial and ethnic groups. Teachers at this level will also want to demonstrate the great variety of methods used in doing similar types of activities. For example, a curriculum can be designed that highlights the many different ways of transporting things, such as carts, wagons, baskets, animals, buckets, or vehicles. Or teachers can use songs and games from various cultures, as well as cooking foods in a variety of ethnically related ways. Rice is a perfect example of a food that is cooked and eaten differently depending on the cultural heritage of the people cooking: some people fry it, some boil it, some steam it, some mix it with other things. The general message that children get from these types of activities is that there are many ways to do similar tasks and that sometimes these ways are influenced by where our families come from.

LEVEL 3: INTEGRATING MULTICULTURAL MATERIALS AND ACTIVITIES INTO THE CURRICULUM

At this level the teacher devotes some focused classroom time to purposeful multicultural education. Teachers who enter at this level have four objectives. First, teachers would begin to talk with parents about multicultural education, as was described in chapter 3. Second, teachers would set aside physical space in the classroom for information on multicultural education. One activity that would meet this objective is designing and building a learning center featuring a multicultural theme, such as "Many Different Kinds of People Live in Our Community"; "We All Have Feelings"; and "There Are Some Ways in Which We All Are Alike; There Are

Some Ways in Which We All Are Different." The third objective for this level is to develop a unit on multicultural education by designing a series of related activities and experiences that focus on affirming cultural differences. All of the examples listed in the preceding levels could be used in a unit approach to multicultural education. At this level, however, the materials and experiences are presented within a specific time frame. This approach is more thorough and organized in the sense that each experience the children have builds upon a preceding experience and suggests future experiences. The children might visit an ethnic grocery store to buy the ingredients to make a particular recipe when they return to the classroom (a detailed description of such a unit is given in chapter 5). The fourth objective of level 3 is to determine to what extent the classroom reflects a multicultural perspective and to strengthen areas that need improvement. Appendix D, "Multicultural Classroom Environment Checklist," can be used for this purpose.

LEVEL 4: DESIGNING A MULTICULTURAL
CLASSROOM ENVIRONMENT

At this level all of the preceding levels are well established, and multicultural education becomes a way of life for teachers and children. At this level the teacher has two primary objectives. The first is to design a learning environment in which children view both their differences as culturally diverse people and their similarities as human beings in a positive way. Doing a language arts activity such as learning to say "Good morning" in English and Spanish underscores the concept that there are some things that everyone does but that the way in which we do them is based in part on cultural heritage. Activities like the one just described fulfill the first objective of this level. The second objective is to provide an environment that encourages children to experience people of diverse cultures working together as unique parts of a whole community. One way to address this objective is for a class to take a walk around the community. While they walk, the teacher can point out the various buildings in a neighborhood: the drug store, the grocery store, the cleaner's, the plumber's, the electrician's, the doctor's office, the police department, the fire station. And she or he can talk about how we need all of these people to make a community work. Just as in the classroom everyone would be hungry if the children whose job it was to put out juice forgot, so people in a community need grocery stores from which to buy their food. There are lots of ways in which people in a community are dependent upon one another. The optimum situation for such a walk is an ethnically diverse community. However, the point of interdependence can be made in either homogeneous or heterogeneous communities. In chapter 6 there is a thorough discussion of designing a multicultural classroom environment.

LEVEL 5: CHANGING THE SCHOOL ENVIRONMENT

At this level the teacher identifies her- or himself as a social change agent within the school system. Objectives for this level are: (1) encouraging the equitable distribution of leadership opportunities and positions within the school; (2) working for a pluralistic power base for the school system; and (3) building support networks for antiracism work within the school and with teachers in other schools. Examples of activities in which a teacher working at level 5 might involve her- or himself are serving on personnel committees that hire staff, working to elect people of color and representatives of community ethnic groups to the school board or board of directors, writing newsletters for area schools, and speaking to community groups.

LEVEL 6: WORKING FOR SOCIAL JUSTICE

At this level the teacher is constantly working in the classroom, in the school system, and in the community on antiracism and social justice issues. She or he might also be involved in national organizations that are working for the elimination of racism, such as the National YWCA. A teacher at this level would campaign for local, state, and national elected officials who support quality child care for all people. She or he would also become involved with organizations working to increase local, state, and federal monies spent on inoculation programs, day-care programs, school lunch programs, and other social services. This involvement would be based on the knowledge that the people who suffer disproportionately from cutbacks are children of color and their families. Finally, a teacher at this level would become a part of a supportive network of people involved not only in the struggle for justice for all people but also in the never-ending battle to rid themselves of their own prejudices and racism.

At every level, teachers need resources from which to get multicultural materials as well as information about specific cultures or about groups doing antiracism work. In appendix C, "Sources for Multicultural Materials," books, pamphlets, and other written materials pertaining to multicultural curriculum development are suggested. A list of organizations and resource centers from which teachers might get multicultural materials is also provided.

# Planning a Resource Unit on Affirming Cultural Diversity 5

The skills and techniques needed for carrying out activities in levels 1 and 2 of multicultural education are generally part of any early childhood training program; there is therefore no need for an in-depth discussion of them here. The skills and techniques needed for level 3, "Integrating Multicultural Materials and Activities Into the Curriculum," however, are less familiar, and since many teachers of young children may be interested in working at this level, this chapter provides some suggestions for developing a unit on affirming cultural diversity. The unit described takes about three weeks to complete; either it can be used in its entirety, or parts of it can be used in designing a multicultural environment.

The unit is an organizational structure used by the teacher in designing curriculum to ensure a balanced, integrated presentation of materials and information to children. It should be emphasized that the unit is a tool for the teacher, not for the children; obviously young children are not able to conceptualize information in such a manner. In planning a unit on any subject, the teacher identifies ideas, skills, attitudes, and values that are integral to a particular concept that she or he would like the children to understand. The

teacher then designs learning activities that support a concrete exploration of the abstract concept at a level developmentally appropriate to the child (Taba, 1962; Taba, Durkin, Fraenkel, &
McNaughton, 1971).

Clearly, young children will not be able to understand the values
and attitudes or the concepts and ideas in the terms in which they
are stated in the unit plan. It is hoped, however, that children will
assimilate the values into their own developing value system and
will grasp some aspects of the basic ideas as they participate in the
learning activities.

## INTRODUCTION OF THE CONCEPT

Young children are, as we have said, appropriately egocentric
and ethnocentric; they see themselves and their own cultural group
as the center of the world. As they develop, their focus begins to
shift from themselves to other people. It is crucial for young chil-

dren to see that there are many different kinds of people in their community and that these different, unique people are what make the community interesting. In order for children to affirm diversity as it pertains to cultural heritages, thoughts, or life-styles, they must have opportunities to experience alternative ways of doing things and opportunities to share and learn from people who are different from themselves.

This unit was developed to provide a multicultural perspective for young children. It focuses on Native American, Asian-American, Spanish-speaking, black, and white people as part of a total community. The goal is not to teach children what each specific culture does but to let them experience cultures working together as unique parts of a hypothetical community.

## Main Idea

Many different cultures work together and contribute their unique qualities to form a strong community.

## Organizing Ideas

A. There are many different kinds of families.
B. All kinds of people live in our community.
C. There are some ways in which we all are alike.
D. There are some ways in which we are different.
E. We work together in our community.

## Skills to Be Developed

In the context of the unit, the children will have the opportunity to develop and utilize the following skills:

| | |
|---|---|
| Observing | Comparing and contrasting |
| Describing | Generalizing |
| Developing concepts | Predicting |
| Sorting | Solving problems |
| Differentiating | Working together |
| Defining | Gathering information |
| Hypothesizing | Explaining |
| Classifying | Offering alternatives |
| Matching | |

## Attitudes and Values to Be Developed

We are all innately, inherently worthy. Our worth is based on our selves, not on someone else's worthlessness.

All human beings are born equal, worthy of respect and dignity, whether they are black, yellow, red, brown, or white; female, or male. Their capabilities are based on their individual drives, desires, opportunities, and education.

We need to value and affirm differences. Each of us is unique and special. Our differences, when joined together in a common task, give our group strength. We grow and learn from experiencing and working with each others' differences and from finding commonalities.

Each of us is an important individual. At the same time, we are all valued members of a group. If we work with other members of our group, we can frequently be more effective than if we worked by ourselves.

The concept of change is a positive one. Although all changes are not necessarily positive, the concept itself is one to be valued.

## UNIT PLAN

**Main Idea:**    Many different cultures work together and contribute their unique qualities to form a strong community.

**Organizing Idea A:**    There are many different kinds of families.

LEARNING ACTIVITIES

1.  Begin by talking with the children about families. Ask the children who they live with. Ask them what members of their family live in other apartments or houses or towns.

    Talk about how people form family groups: children are born to parents, children are adopted, people come together out of love and necessity.

    Talk about the fact that everyone has a family, but there are lots of different kinds of families: mother-child, mother-father-child/children, grandparents-child/children, grandparents-parents-child/children, older sibling caring for younger children, extended families including aunts, uncles, cousins in the primary group, and so on. Remember to include family pets.

2. Provide magazine pictures of a variety of people. Try to find examples of people resembling family members of the children in the class, such as grandmothers, aunts, cousins, mothers, fathers, siblings, family pets. Ask the children to build a family portrait using the magazine pictures. The children will probably use their own family as a framework on which to base their picture. Display all of these pictures, *at the children's eye level*, in the group meeting place.

Talk with the children about what they see in the pictures. How do all of the people look alike? How do they look different?

3. Find lots of pictures in magazines of all kinds of families; mount and laminate some and put them on the wall or bulletin board, *at the children's eye level*, for them to look at and enjoy. Include all major cultural groups and all sorts of family configurations. Mount and laminate other pictures and use them in group discussions and various learning activities. For example, ask children to find the family with two sisters, or with a father, or with a grandmother and grandfather. Through such an activity children will become aware of the wide variety of families.

4. Provide blank books for each child to use in making a book about his or her family. Since the children are not yet able to read or write, they can dictate stories to the teacher.

Encourage the children to put whatever they want to about their families in their books, for example, stories about deaths, divorces, and births as well as everyday occurrences.

5. Make a new-word chart of words children use to describe how their families look, what they do, and so on. (Even though the children are unable to read, if they help the teacher put the words on the chart and look at it every day, they will soon remember what the words are. Part of the reading readiness process is learning that the spoken word can be written down.)

6.   Take the children on a trip around the neighborhood. Let them show their friends where they live. Show them where the teacher lives. Talk about who lives in their house or apartment. Talk about who lives on their block. Do old people live on the block? Are there lots of children? Ask them what sorts of buildings, stores, animals, people, growing things they saw on one block that they did not see on another. Make a list of what is seen while on the trip.

   After returning to the classroom, make a language experience chart about the trip by writing next to each child's name a comment by the child about the experience. Using the list made on the trip, count how many dogs or grocery stores or stop signs were seen. Ask the children to dictate stories about the trip.

7.   Invite the children to build the neighborhood with blocks. Put labels on the buildings, including signs showing where the children live.

8.   Talk about what the adult members of the children's families do with their time. Make language experience charts based on this discussion.

   In order to support all children's life experiences, remember that parents or other family members who are not working outside the home are doing useful things at home, such as housework and caring for children. Include these jobs in the language experience charts.

9.   Repeat the above activity, focusing on what children do with their time. Do they have jobs in the classroom; do they have jobs at home?

10.   Talk about what families do when they play. What do they do as a whole family? What do they do alone? What do some family members do together that is special? For example, grandparent and child walk to school each day, brother and sister build forts together, mother or father and child work in the garden or play in the park.

11.   Ask the children what songs their families sing together. Let them teach the songs to the other children.

12.   What kinds of routines does each family have? How are these routines alike from family to family? How are they different? How are the routines like the ones at school—for example, brushing teeth after meals, and setting tables?

13. Ask the children what their favorite foods are. Locate recipes of the children's favorite foods. If possible, have parents come to school to cook with the children. How are the foods that the children eat at home different from one another? How are they alike?

    Make a recipe book, including pictures of the foods, if possible.

    Invite families to eat breakfast or lunch with the children. Let the children cook the food for the families, using recipes from their recipe books.

14. Put out the people block accessories in the block corner. Make new family block accessories by attaching a magazine picture or a photograph of a person to an appropriate-sized block, making sure that you have multicultural, nonsexist accessories that do not reinforce racial or sex stereotypes.

15. Make simple graphs about the number of children in each child's family, number of pets, number of people in each family, number of boys, number of girls, and so on.

16. Change the housekeeping area so that it represents different kinds of homes, by putting up different curtains, different pictures on the wall, and so on. Have a wide variety of dress-up clothes available for the children: various ethnic clothes, various occupation-related clothes, clothes that parents might wear, clothes that grandparents might wear. Since dramatic play provides an opportunity for children to try on a variety of roles, all children should feel free to wear any of the clothes regardless of the sex role or gender suggested by the clothes themselves.

17. Provide materials for the children to use in drawing or painting pictures of their families. Older children might enjoy stitching a simple family sampler that they have designed.

18. To consolidate this part of the unit, review with the children the work that they have done on families. Do a language experience chart that will help you assess what the children learned about how families are the same or how they are different.

    Make a big mural or collage using pictures the children have drawn.

19. To begin the transition from families to people in the community, talk about how all of the children's families together

form a group of people, people who live together and work and play together, people who are all part of the same community.

## Organizing Idea B:    All kinds of people live in our community.

LEARNING ACTIVITIES

1.  To acquaint the children with the concept of community, draw on the work that has been done on families. Point out that family members all do their part to keep the household running, just as each child in the classroom does her or his job to see that everything is taken care of at school. A community is a group of people who live near each other and can work together in ways that are helpful to everybody.

    Have the children look at the mural or collage they made toward the end of their work on families. Point out to them that the people whose pictures are on the mural form a community.

2.  Make a cozy area in the room where children can sit quietly. Put up pictures of people from a large variety of cultures, being sure to include pictures of people of all ages. Put a pillow in the cozy area to encourage the children to sit and look at the pictures.

3.  Make a mobile of pictures of children's faces, representing many cultures. Hang the mobile in the cozy area so that the children can see it while they are in the area. Ask the children how the people in the pictures on the wall and in the mobile look different from each other and how they look the same.

4.  Introduce a filmstrip, such as *Who Am I?* (Scholastic Magazine, Inc., 1972), that presents in a developmentally appropriate manner children from a variety of racial and ethnic groups. Talk about all the different children in it and what they are doing.

5.  Talk with the children about who lives in their community. They will probably mention a variety of community workers as well as their own families and their friends' families. Make a language experience chart listing all of the community workers,

being careful to use nonsexist terms for the workers, such as:

police officer      salesperson
fire fighter      milk carrier
newspaper carrier

Put pictures by some of the names of the community workers. As the children meet more people in the community, add their names or functions to the "People in Our Community" language experience chart.

Invite the children to dictate stories about the jobs of the community workers and to illustrate their stories. Combine their stories and make a class book. (See learning activity 8.)

6. Take trips to see the community workers at their jobs. Include in your selection of community workers members of a variety of ethnic, racial, and cultural groups. In addition to having them find out what these people do, talk with the children about how each of these people helps the whole community work better. If the class is unable to take trips to see community workers, invite workers to the classroom to talk with the children about their jobs.

7. On trips around the school neighborhood, note how many businesses are in the community. (If your school is isolated from the center of the city, visit the central business district, if that is feasible.) Take pictures of the stores and the buildings.

In the block corner, encourage the children to make a simple model of the business district of their neighborhood. The first step in this process is to make a language experience chart or write stories about the neighborhood the children visited. Put the pictures you took of the buildings up on the wall in the block corner, at the children's eye level, so that they can use them as guides for their buildings. (Four- and five-year-olds who have built in the block corner a lot should not have any trouble with this task. Younger children or children who have not built much will have to simplify the task to suit their building skills.)

8. Ask the children to keep a book on "People in Our Community." This can be a class project with each child contributing a dictated story, or children can make their own books.

9.  To begin the transition from talking about community to talk-
    ing about ways in which people are all alike, ask the children to
    name all of the people whom they have put on the "People in
    Our Community" language experience chart or about whom
    they have dictated stories in their community book. Get them
    to think about ways in which all these people are alike: they all
    wear clothes, they all eat food, they all live in houses or apart-
    ments, they all work, they all play.

**Organizing Idea C:**   There are some ways in which we all
are alike.

LEARNING ACTIVITIES

These activities focus on five ways in which all people are alike:

    We all eat.
    We all work.
    We all play.
    We all live in some sort of dwelling.
    We all wear clothes.

The essential ingredient for this section of the unit is lots and lots of pictures. Raid the picture file, and supplement it with pictures from magazines that focus on red, yellow, brown, and black people. In most instances you will want to mount them on poster board and laminate them, but it is a good idea to decide which activities you are going to use them for before mounting them, since you may want to color-coordinate a group of pictures for a specific learning activity. Choose pictures that show one of these five categories: people eating, people working, people playing, clothes people wear, or people's dwellings. When choosing pictures of dwellings, use pictures that are not so different from the children's experience that they take on a "foreign" or "exotic" air.

1.  To introduce this part of the unit, show the children a collection of pictures depicting all kinds of people eating, working, wearing clothes, playing, or living in their respective dwellings. Talk to them about what the people are doing. Try to provide opportunities for children to try the things they are seeing in the pictures. Ask questions about the pictures, taking care to point out things the children might have missed.

2.  Make a sorting game using two to five pictures from each of the five categories listed above (ten to twenty-five total). Make a big pocket chart out of fabric or a set of manila envelopes pasted onto poster board and put picture and word labels under each pocket; for example, the label would say, "We all eat," and on the label would be a simple picture of a person eating.

    Explain the game to the children: "Sort the pictures by putting each one into the pocket where you think it should go. Look at the pictures on the labels to tell you what group of pictures goes in each pocket. When you have finished sorting, we will talk about how you choose which pocket to put each picture in. Lots of the pictures could go in more than one pocket."

3.  Make matching lotto games using pictures of dwellings, people eating, or clothes people wear.

4.  In the block corner put up pictures of various sorts of dwellings and encourage the children to build structures like those they see in the pictures.

5.  Put books in the quiet area that deal with one or more of the

ways in which we are all alike. (See appendix A, "Bibliography of Multicultural Children's Books," for suggestions.)

6.  Make puzzles for your manipulative materials that are related to one or more of the five categories. Magazine pictures can be glued to cardboard, laminated, and cut into sections or strips for the children to reassemble.

**Organizing Idea D:**    There are some ways in which we are different. The purpose of this section is to help children understand that there are some things we all do but that the ways in which we do them vary according to what we learn in our families. Children will begin to get a sense of cultural heritage and its effects on our actions and our approaches to the way in which we live our lives.

LEARNING ACTIVITIES

These activities focus on five areas in which people do things differently:

    Cooking
    Making music
    Celebrating a holiday
    Carrying out a daily routine
    Talking together

1.  Introduce this section by sharing with the children several books showing a culturally different child doing one of the things listed above.

    Ask the children what is happening in the books. Ask them if they have ever done what the child in the books is doing. Let the children share their experiences with you. When possible, do the activities the children see in the book.

### Cooking

2.  Make a cookbook with the children. Include ethnic recipes as well as simple recipes from cookbooks. (You might want to add these recipes to the collection begun in the first section of this unit rather than making a new cookbook.)

3.  Each cooking experience should begin with a trip to the grocery store, if it is at all feasible. Two or three children and a teacher can make the shopping list, buy the ingredients, and

bring them back to use in cooking. Letting the children help to buy the foods not only gives them a better sense of what the cooking process involves but also gives them the opportunity to see where food comes from before it gets to their homes.

Ask parents to cook with you and the children or just to join you when the children are cooking something new and different.

### Music

4.  Teach the children all sorts of songs, and let them teach songs to their classmates.
5.  Listen to music from various cultures. Sing songs, play records, and take children to neighborhood musical events. Use these experiences to help children identify and label the feelings that music inspires, such as joy, peace, and excitement. Encourage children to move with the music, clap hands in time to the music, use rhythm sticks along with the music. Tap out a rhythm and invite children to repeat it, using hands, feet, or sticks.
6.  Introduce new musical instruments from different cultures to the children. Instruments such as reed pipes, bongo drums, castanets, or maracas are interesting and fun. For some suggestions on making rhythm instruments, see *Resources for Creative Teaching in Early Childhood Education* (Flemming, Hamilton, & Hicks, 1977).

### Holidays

7.  Historically, schools in the United States have fallen into an ethnocentric trap regarding holiday celebrations. Only recently have schools begun to celebrate holidays other than the ones promoted by white Christians. Although most three-, four-, and five-year-olds cannot really understand the concept that people live in other countries, they are able to understand, for example, that some people celebrate Christmas and some celebrate Hanukkah.

    Taking a multicultural approach to the issue of holiday celebrations requires two primary commitments:
    a.  To celebrate holidays honored by various cultures, giving them equal importance in the curriculum.

b.   To provide children with simple, honest, historical ac-
counts of the bases for these holiday celebrations. For
example, on Columbus Day, *don't* tell the children Columbus discovered America. He didn't. Tell them he was
a famous explorer who sailed across the ocean from far
away and landed at a place he called America. Be sure to
tell them that when he came here there were Native
Americans who had been living in America for a long
time.

   For an extensive and useful description of culturally diverse holiday celebrations, see the section on "Family
Celebrations" in *Resources for Creative Teaching in Early
Childhood Education* (Flemming, Hamilton, & Hicks, 1977).
Also see "Beyond 'Ten Little Indians' and Turkeys—Alternative Approaches to Thanksgiving," an article by Patricia Ramsey in the September 1979 issue of *Young Children*.

## Daily Routine

8.   Even our simplest actions, such as many of our daily routines,
reflect our cultural heritage. The order in which we eat our
food, the ways we hold our eating implements, when and how
we bathe, and how we wash, dry, and fold clothes are all
partially shaped by our culture. Thus it is important for
teachers to be sensitive to their own ways of carrying out daily
routines as well as being aware of the children's ways of doing
things. For example, many white middle-class Americans set a
table by putting the fork to the left of the plate and the knife
and spoon to the right, while some Puerto Rican people set the
table the opposite way. In our ethnocentric way, it would be all
too possible to think that the Puerto Rican child who set the
table with the fork on the right and the knife and spoon on the
left was simply making a mistake.

## Talking Together

9.   The way we speak and the language we speak is greatly determined by our cultural heritage. Because of their egocentricity
and ethnocentricity, young children who speak English in this

country never think about the fact that not everyone uses English as her or his first language.

Find books that are written in two languages, such as English and Spanish, or English and Swahili. (See appendix A, "Bibliography of Multicultural Children's Books," for suggestions.) Read them to the children. Talk about the language in the book; ask them to listen to the sounds of the words. Ask them if they can understand the words in the new language. How does it make them feel not to be able to understand the words?

If you are fortunate enough to have one or more children in your classroom who speak a language other than English, be sure to encourage the English-speaking children to learn that language, too, as you are asking the children who speak another language to learn English. In this way the English-speaking children understand how difficult it is not to speak the primary language, and the non-English-speaking children have the satisfaction of sharing the ways in which they communicate within their own culture with their English-speaking friends.

**Organizing Idea E:**   We work together in our community. This section is the culmination of the unit. The purpose of the section is to help children see that we are all alike in some ways but that it is our differences that make us unique and special. If we work together and share those unique characteristics, we can learn from one another and grow with one another.

LEARNING ACTIVITIES

1.  Make a class book. Include in it a collection of stories and pictures of people doing things with people of different cultural heritages.
2.  Make a big class mural. When it is finished it will be an example of the work that gets done when all of the children work together.
3.  Make a language experience chart with a list of all of the activities in the unit the children can remember.
4.  Talk with the children about the unit. Go back over the groups of activities associated with each organizing idea. Look at the stories and the mural and the work that took place during the

unit to see if you think the children understood the basic goals of the unit. What aspect of the unit did the children like best? What part did they least enjoy?

## EVALUATION

Evaluation is the process by which teachers assess children's progress in their work or their understanding of an experience, an idea, or a concept. Through evaluation teachers can also measure the success of their own presentation or organization of material or of a given lesson. Evaluation is an ongoing, never-ending process. In a preschool classroom the teacher constantly notes children's responses to each other, to the teacher, to the work, and to the environment. Sometimes this process is formal: teachers can identify the milestones in a child's growth by recording observations and keeping school records. Some of a teacher's evaluation of a child's growth is informal: through interactions with the child or through casual conversations with parents about how a child is doing at home, the teacher gains information that reveals developmental changes.

The evaluation of the unit on affirming cultural diversity is similar to the rest of the evaluation that goes on in a classroom. Formal evaluation includes recording how children work on or approach suggested activities. Children's verbal responses to questions concerned with cultural diversity or the nature of their responses to people who are culturally different (both in and out of the classroom) help a teacher evaluate the child's understanding of the unit. Further, formal evaluation is built into the activities themselves. Since many activities in this unit build on previous activities and prepare the children for future ones, the teacher can evaluate her or his ordering of experiences by watching the children's reaction to each new activity. If the children are confused or unable to contribute, the teacher knows that she or he must provide more experiences at a different level or in a different way before children can do well at the next level. Informal evaluation takes the form of noting the level of the children's involvement in the activities. The combination of formal and informal aspects of evaluation can give the teacher a good deal of information about the success of the unit as a whole.

Clearly, young children will not be able to understand the values and attitudes or the concepts and ideas in the terms in which they are stated in the unit plan. It is hoped, however, that children will assimilate the values into their own developing value system and will grasp some aspects of the basic ideas as they participate in the learning activities. Because the unit is organized into sequential and related learning activities, each concept and idea is presented in a variety of ways. By using the unit as a model for curriculum planning rather than using a less organized or structured approach, there is a greater chance that these values and concepts will be incorporated into the child's thinking.

# Developing
# a Multicultural Classroom
# Environment _____ 6

Designing a multicultural classroom environment requires a very high level of involvement in multicultural education. At this stage, the teacher is ready to adopt a multicultural perspective in all aspects of the curriculum, in the physical environment, and in her or his own approach to the education of young children. Just as a curriculum reflects the system of values of its creator, curriculum materials reflect the attitudes of the person or people who choose materials to be used in the classroom. The pictures on the walls, the books on the shelves, the dolls in the dramatic play area, and the records in the music area will all reflect the diverse nature of a multicultural community in a classroom environment designed by a teacher committed to a multicultural approach.

The six primary aspects of the learning environment for young children discussed in this chapter are language arts, social studies, blocks, dramatic play, music and games, and cooking. While science and mathematics are not formally addressed, concepts and activities from both of these subject areas are integrated into descriptions of other aspects of the learning environment.

## LANGUAGE ARTS

Books and language-experience activities frequently take up a large part of the child's day in preschool. Using multicultural

guidelines in choosing books and activities greatly facilitates the entire multicultural program. Through books and language-experience activities like group discussions, children have the opportunity to go beyond the boundaries of their own environment and to increase their understanding of and sensitivity to other people's lives.

### Guidelines

The following guidelines for choosing books and other materials for language arts (such as magazines, books with records and tapes, records of stories and folk tales, books of poems, or simply stories told to children) are meant as suggestions rather than hard and fast rules. Teachers can evaluate language arts materials with the following questions in mind. (Teachers will be able to add other guidelines as they increase their own sensitivity to cultural diversity.)

How are differences in skin color, life-styles, or value systems treated? Are characters with skin colors, value systems, or life-styles other than white and middle class presented in a positive light?

Are the characters drawn in a way that encourages children of diverse backgrounds to identify with them and care about them?

Are children depicted as working together, each bringing her or his special skills and qualities to a situation?

Look at the street scenes, the playground and classroom scenes: how different are the children from one another? Could most children identify with the picture?

Look at the role casting of the characters: are the interests and abilities stereotyped according to the color or sex of the person?

How do authority figures interact with children? Is there mutual respect on the part of both groups?

How do children reading the books see adult minority figures in the books? What roles do adult minority people play?

What is the vocabulary of the book? Look carefully at the use of words such as *black* and *white*. Is *black* associated with negative things? Look carefully at the use of dialect. Is it genuine or is it fabricated?

Are picture books depicting historical situations written from a white viewpoint? Are Indians presented as savages? Do all the minority people look alike? Is Columbus discussed as the discoverer of America?

Clearly, if teachers applied all of these guidelines in the assessment of each book or other language arts material, they would have to dispose of the majority of their collections. There are, however, a couple of less drastic ways to deal with this problem. First, one can focus on removing particularly offensive materials from the classroom. Books such as Helen Bannerman's *Little Black Sambo*, for instance, rely so heavily on racial stereotypes, such as the idea of black people wearing "loud" clothes, that it is impossible to sort out any information that might be true. Because young children are not developmentally able to distinguish between what is true and what is not true, they take the stereotype misinformation as fact. Second, the teacher can talk to children about the books that are being read and ask them what they think about the stories. Ezra Jack Keats's *The Snowy Day*, for example, has received a great deal of criticism for its presentation of the black mother. She is described as big and warm, and she looks like the stereotype that white culture perpetuates of black mothers. The teacher might ask the black children in the class if their mothers look like the one in the picture. The teacher could also ask how their mothers are the same and how they are different from this mother. In a class that does not include black children, one can ask if the mother in the story looks like the mother in another book about a black family. In this way the children are encouraged to think about what they are seeing rather than simply taking the picture as truly representative of all black women. Such an imaginative approach to other picture books can enhance the learning value of language arts materials that do not meet all of the criteria of the multicultural guidelines.

## The Use of Language in Language Arts Materials

In the United States, we place great importance on how articulate one is, on the caliber of English one speaks, and on the way one expresses oneself. A large measure of racism is built into our vocabulary, just as it is built into all other areas of our lives. Racism also carries over into the language in which children's books are written. In the preface of *We Build Together* (1967), Charlamae Rollins discusses the use of dialect in books for children. She observes that it is neither correct nor fair to portray black people as always speaking in dialect and maintains that for the author to create a "false idiom" or to make up a dialect using words such as "dat" and "dem" is racist. She does point out, however, that we all speak in some dialect and that to write in the dialect that is our own gives the reader a better sense of the characters in the story. She urges that "just as stereotyped portrayal of the Negro must be replaced by a sensitive, accurate portrayal, so the caricature of his language should be replaced by accurate, understandable use of the vernacular" (p. xv). Recent books for young children that portray black experiences in America have moved a long way toward Rollins's goals of sensitive and accurate portrayal. (For suggestions, see "Bibliography of Multicultural Children's Books," appendix A.)

### Diversity of Materials

Supplying a variety of different language arts materials and experiences is another aspect of the multicultural approach to the curriculum. Children can learn about cultures other than their own by simply looking at pictures from ethnic magazines such as *Essence*, *Ebony*, or *Jet*, or at travel magazines. Teachers need to beware of magazines like *National Geographic Magazine* that frequently present people of color as strange or exotic. Folk tales provide an enormous amount of insight into a group's cultural heritage; poems from various cultures give children a sense of how different people use language and words. In short, the greater the cultural variety of pre-reading and listening experiences children have, the more likely the children are to affirm differences in others and to be willing to share their own uniqueness.

## SOCIAL STUDIES

As teachers of young children know, one of the chief purposes of putting young children in a group situation such as a nursery school, a day-care center, or a preschool is to help them learn to be social beings. In fact, developing social skills is a major component in the young child's day of play and work. Social studies is that part of a preschool curriculum that concentrates on helping children develop human relations. Social studies cannot be confined to one specific learning area or set time in a school day; social education goes on all the time in the classroom. Children are constantly trying to figure themselves out, both in a self-centered manner and in relation to other people and objects in their environment.

The concept of social studies is inherently multicultural. Social studies concerns itself with preparing children to enter into diverse intergroup relations, as well as with giving them skills and knowledge needed to function in an increasingly changing world. Part of the rationale for a social studies curriculum is to help children increase their understanding and acceptance of attitudes, values, and life-styles that are unfamiliar to them.

In developing a social studies curriculum for young children, it is important to remember that they are first and foremost concerned with themselves and their immediate surroundings. While a social studies curriculum for older children often examines communities far away and studies the ways in which other cultures deal with their environment, the teacher of young children needs to structure an environment in which the children can learn about themselves and each other as social beings. Within a classroom environment that encourages children to feel good about themselves individually and to begin to sort out their own relations to the people in their immediate surroundings, it is also the teacher's job to provide the children with ongoing multicultural experiences. In a culturally heterogeneous class, this multicultural experience will include immediate contact with children of other cultural backgrounds. In a monocultural setting, regardless of the culture represented, it is especially important that the teacher provide a hypothetical multicultural environment through thoughtful selection of curriculum materials and learning activities that reflect a multicultural society. In this way younger children will be better prepared for diverse experiences as they grow older.

When selecting curriculum materials, teachers need to guard against racial, ethnic, and sex role stereotypes as well as against ethnocentricity. Books and other materials are often racially stereotypic. Native Americans are depicted as living in tepees, wearing feathers, war paint, and loin cloths, and saying "Ugh." They are called "braves" or "Heap Big Chief" or "Little Red" instead of Indian names. Sexual stereotypes creep in, too: women are depicted only as mothers and care givers, while men have a variety of exciting tasks. (This is especially true with learning materials that focus on community helpers.) Too often the world is presented from a white, middle-class American point of view; for example, stories may describe families as consisting of mother, father, and two children, and other family configurations are implicitly seen as less than adequate. Cultural differences such as styles of dress or foods eaten are presented as foreign, quaint, or exotic. Presenting material in this manner encourages intolerance rather than openness in children. Designing a curriculum that is inclusive rather than exclusive is crucial. Through a curriculum that affirms diversity in people, thoughts, and actions, children will be better prepared to cope with situations and experiences that are new and different.

# UNIT BLOCKS

Building with unit blocks is frequently a large part of the early childhood curriculum. Developed by Caroline Pratt in the early 1900s, unit blocks are a medium through which the child can recreate her or his own experience. Pratt saw blocks as the most basic learning tool in a curriculum; they are still used as such in the school she founded in New York City (Hirsch, 1974). Unit blocks have no color and no guiding design, so the child controls what she or he builds and how. "Working with blocks contributes to the physical, social, cognitive, and emotional development of children. To put it more succinctly, blocks complement the development of the *whole* child" (Sprung, 1975, pp. 35–36).

There are four primary stages of block play: (1) solitary play; (2) parallel play; (3) associative play; and (4) cooperative play (Hirsch, 1974). In solitary play, the child explores the materials; she or he sets up a relationship with them to see how they will and won't work, what they will and won't do. When the child is comfortable with the blocks, she or he moves on to parallel play. During the parallel play stage, children work side by side building their own buildings. Sometimes they talk to each other, but they do not share ideas about what to build or how to solve a building problem. There is some duplicating of other children's work at this stage; a child is eager to know if a building that balances for another child is going to balance for her or him as well.

The third stage in the development of block building is associative play. At this stage each child first builds his or her own buildings, but then the children join their buildings together to form a larger project. For example, one child might work on an airport, and one child might work on an airplane hangar. They would then join the buildings with runways that they would work on together. In this way the planes could taxi into the airport, leave the passengers at the terminal, and taxi on to the hangar. The final stage of block play is cooperative play in which several children work together on a whole project. Regardless of their age, children go through these four stages. The speed at which a child goes through the stages depends on her or his age as well as her or his learning style. Playing with blocks reinforces the goals of multicultural education by allowing for a variety of learning styles, by encouraging cooperative play, and by providing opportunities for children to work interdependently.

Unit blocks can be used very productively as a primary learning tool with children from one-and-a-half to eight or nine years old. With very young children (two years and younger), it is best to put a fairly small number of blocks out initially and work up to about one half a set for ten two-year-olds. Simple shapes, such as half units, units, and double units, are most useful (Hirsch, 1974, p. 105). Three-, four-, and five-year-olds do lots of dramatic play in the block corner. Their building increases in complexity as the children become less egocentric. Just at the stage when children begin to put more details in drawings, their block buildings become more elaborate. The buildings have doors, windows, and roofs. Six-, seven-, and eight-year-olds do very sophisticated building, making cities, farms, communities with electric lights, buildings with elevators, and bridges. For older children, working with blocks is a very good way to begin acquiring map-making skills. In *Young Geographers* (1971), Lucy Sprague Mitchell talks about map skills and blocks. This book is a wonderful resource for teachers working with elementary school children on geography, social studies, or science.

Children learn new concepts and increase their skills in science, mathematics, social studies, and language through block building. Concepts such as equilibrium, balance, gravity, seriation and order, proximity, vertical and horizontal, up and down, and inside and outside can all be addressed using blocks. Children practice skills in classifying, comparing, predicting, and hypothesizing as well as sorting according to shape, size, weight, length, or height in the block corner. In terms of social studies, the block area offers many opportunities for cooperation and socialization. Children can also use blocks to recreate structures they have seen on a trip, thereby making the trip experience far more real and meaningful. Language arts activities play a large part in block building. Before building something that has been seen on a trip, the teacher and children make a language chart telling what they saw, what it looked like, and what they thought about it. The block construction site needs lots of signs explaining what the building is, who built it, and what it is used for. Following the building, the children may write or dictate stories about what they have done. Thus three types of language arts experiences develop from one trip to see a building.

Block corner accessories can also reflect a multicultural perspective. The people block accessories can mirror a hypothetical multicultural community, so that children are helped to develop a culturally diverse frame of reference. Community helpers and family members can be multiracial and nonstereotypic in terms of race or sex roles.

In addition to the people accessories, other accessories for the block area include trucks, buses, boats, airplanes, cars, trains, farm animals, zoo animals, dinosaurs, puppets, batteries and bulbs to light the buildings, pulleys, string, tape and paper and crayons for descriptive signs and scenery. With two-, three-, and four-year-olds, it is best to use fewer accessories than with five- and six-year-olds. Otherwise the younger children will concentrate more on the accessories and less on the blocks.

Unfortunately the block corner is frequently seen as the boys' domain; girls simply are not welcome there. Teachers can help to discourage this tendency by encouraging girls to work with blocks. The block area might be placed next to the housekeeping or dramatic play area. Boys and girls are then more likely to explore both areas by combining their dramatic play activity with block building. Girls are as good builders as boys, and they deserve every opportunity to enjoy the block corner.

Block building has limitless possibilities, but if teachers are not comfortable with the blocks, the children probably will not be either. The teacher can profitably spend some time alone building with blocks. She or he might photograph children working together in the block corner, display photographs of their buildings, and make a book of the photograph collection for the reading or library area. The more teachers enjoy and appreciate building, the better the children will feel about devoting their energies to blocks and the more they will learn.

# DRAMATIC PLAY

Dramatic play is one of the most important aspects of the young child's curriculum, and it has enormous potential in a classroom that is multicultural. Through dramatic play children are able to try on many different roles and behaviors to see how they fit, without committing themselves to being one thing or another; an aggressive child can be vulnerable and soft, a shy child can be bold and brave. In the dramatic play area, children can practice behaviors they have seen in the adults around them. They can safely work out their feelings about what goes on at home, making up alternative solutions to problems they have encountered. During dramatic play, three-year-olds can be babies or they can be adults, without anyone's telling them they are silly. Children are also able to explore, at their own developmental levels, what it feels like to belong to another culture, through the concrete experiences of wearing clothes from a different culture or working in a housekeeping area that is set up differently than their own homes are.

In order for children to use the dramatic play area most advantageously, the roles available within the area should not be limited by ethnocentricity or sex role stereotypes. No one cultural group should be overrepresented either in the pictures on the walls or in the overall atmosphere of the area. In many classrooms the dramatic play area is basically a kitchen/eating area and a bedroom. If there is enough space, the teacher can add a living room so that children can sit down and talk to one another, either as they see grown-ups do at home or as they would like to see grown-ups do. Canvas curtains and striped bedspreads can be used in the bedroom instead of lace, pastel colors, and flowery prints, to avoid a stereotypically feminine atmosphere. A comfortable lounge chair and a rocking chair as well as a table and chairs for use at mealtime might be included. It is also good to change the area around from time to time so that it represents styles of living in various cultures. For example, a mat might be put on the floor to use as a bed or a hammock might be slung to help children understand that different people have different ways of sleeping.

When the clothes in the dramatic play area are neatly stored and well organized, the children know where to find things initially as well as where to put things back when they are finished with them.

Including clothes from several cultures, such as a kimono and a dashiki, gives children the additional opportunity of learning the proper names for these garments as well as allowing them to experience wearing clothes of a different culture. The children need work clothes as well as fancy clothes, everyday shoes as well as dressy shoes. One might provide all sorts of women's and men's clothes, not just suits or jackets worn by white-collar workers. For example, a work shirt makes a fine construction worker's uniform. It is also a good idea to have overalls or painter's pants, using sizes that are not too big for children or cutting the clothes down to size so that they won't fall off the children or trip them. Every kind of hat imaginable can go into the dramatic play area: a miner's hat, a baseball cap, scarves, turbans. In addition to clothes, children love to play with pieces of cloth; they can make them into capes, robes, sashes, dresses, or tablecloths. Just a few pieces of cloth can add many new dimensions to the clothes collection.

In her book *Non-Sexist Education for Young Children*, Barbara Sprung (1975) reported that having more briefcases and fewer purses in the dramatic play area encouraged boys and girls to do more dramatic play about going to work. In addition to briefcases, one can supply other work props such as lunch boxes, backpacks, or big canvas bags that can be used as mail-carrier pouches, grocery bags, or carrying bags. Finally, one can include clothes that are appropriate for older people, as well as clothes for parent-aged people and for children. Anything is possible in dramatic play, so children's imaginations should be stimulated rather than limited by the props available for their use.

Since dolls are "one of the first abstract symbols used by children to replace the self as an object of play" (Sprung, 1975, p. 30), they are extremely valuable in helping children develop a strong self-concept. Providing a wide selection of multiracial dolls in the dramatic play area therefore seems critical. In the classroom both boys and girls need dolls that look like them, as well as dolls that look like other children in the community. In a homogeneous class a multiracial selection of dolls encourages children to engage in hypothetical interactions with people of color. Through observing this play, teachers are able to gain information about how the children in the class perceive other racial groups. In a heterogeneous class the dolls become a reflection of the class community. When selecting the dolls, the teacher will want to avoid black, brown, red, or yellow ones that have exactly the same features as the white ones except for the skin color and will choose those that authentically represent the facial characteristics of various people of color.

In short, the dramatic play area is one of the most crucial in the classroom. It represents, for some children, a microcosm of the world, a space in which they can be in control of a situation as they see adults in control outside the dramatic play area. For other children it is an opportunity to move from the all too real world to one in which life is not so hard. Irrespective of the purposes it serves for children, the dramatic play area needs to have items in it that are culturally diverse in order to be inviting to all children, regardless of color or sex.

# MUSIC AND GAMES

Taking a multicultural approach to music and games not only is easy but is lots of fun. All it takes is a commitment to more careful selection of games and music, keeping in mind the goal of overall cultural diversity in the materials presented in the classroom. It is important to talk to the children about the music they listen to and sing as well as about the games they play, so that they are aware that different cultural groups, or "kinds of people," listen to different kinds of music and play different games. By using culturally diverse music and games, the children are learning, in a small way, about other people's lives.

## Music

There is available for children a lot of music that particularly reflects the cultures from which it stems; for example, folk songs have been recorded from virtually every ethnic group in this country. So that children can get a sense of music from other countries as well, simple songs sung in languages other than English can be included in the collection of records and tapes in the listening area. The best source for culturally diverse music, in terms of variety and availability, is Folkways Records.

It is good to have a listening area in the classroom with records and a record player, or tapes and a cassette recorder, and a set of earphones. Some five-year-olds may be able to work with the equipment themselves; otherwise the teacher must be responsible for changing records or tapes. If there is enough space, the listening area can be made soft and cozy with a pillow or two and can be partitioned off so that it is somewhat removed from the rest of the classroom. If the teacher values this area and transmits this message to the children by the way the area is arranged, the children will see the listening area as an integral part of their work, not just somewhere to go when the "real work" is finished. Children will also enjoy time in the day for singing and listening to music in a large group. Most young children love to sing with their friends, so it does not take too much encouragement to produce a rousing chorus.

Another way to enjoy music besides listening to it and singing it is to make it. The children can easily make a variety of inexpensive percussion instruments, such as two paper cups taped together open end to open end with pebbles inside, or two blocks of wood with sandpaper glued on them for rubbing together. Children can also make their own musical instruments, using instruments from other cultures as models. For example, they can make an instrument that resembles a maraca by putting dried pumpkin seeds in a paper cup, covering the top of the cup with a piece of paper and taping the paper to the sides of the cup. Before the children make maracas, the teacher can show them real ones and talk about how some children use maracas to make music. The teacher could also read a book to the children about Spanish-speaking children making music. (Suggestions of children's books are cited in appendix A, "Bibliography of Multicultural Children's Books.") Lots of everyday household items can be used as instruments: spoons (wooden and metal), combs, an old metal washboard, pots and pans, or glasses filled with different amounts of water. Instruments that are available commercially, such as castanets or triangles, add variety to musical experiences. In short, there is no end to the musical instruments the children can make for very little money, and with some guidance from the teacher they can spend many hours exploring cultural diversity through music.

## Games

Playing games is a universal activity for children. Games are different from play, because games have rules and play does not. Games offer children the opportunity to measure their skills without losing face if they do not win. Iona and Peter Opie, in *Children's Games in Street and Playground* (1969), write about what games do for children:

> In games a child can exert himself without having to explain himself, he can be a good player without having to think if he is a popular person, he can find himself being a useful partner to someone of whom he is ordinarily afraid. He can be confident, too, in particular games, that it is his place to issue commands, to inflict pain, to steal people's possessions, to pretend to be dead, to hurl a ball actually at someone, to pounce on someone, to kiss someone he has caught. In ordinary life he either never knows these experiences or, by attempting them, makes himself an outcast. . . . When a child plays a game he creates a situation which is under his control, and yet it is one of which he does not know the outcome. (p. 3)

These authors go on to say that children today play games that were played hundreds, and in some cases, thousands of years ago. Each successive generation of children believes it has created the games. Further, children all over the world play many of the same games with only minor changes made from culture to culture.

Applying a multicultural approach to the games that are played in a classroom requires much the same kind of ingenuity necessary for using culturally diverse music in the curriculum. Teachers can do two things: call on the ethnic resources within the school community, and do research to find age-appropriate games played by children of various cultural heritages. (Suggestions for such resources are listed in appendix C, "Sources for Multicultural Materials.") In a heterogeneous classroom the children themselves are sources for games played in their respective cultures. The sharing of games will not only be a source of enjoyment but also a way to give the children a better understanding of their friends' ethnic heritages. Young children are not developmentally ready to play games that are complex or have lots of rules. Even a game as simple as hopscotch is frustrating for a three-year-old who can barely hop on one foot or a four-year-old who does not yet know the number sequence from one to ten. Finger plays or very simple gamelike activities are suitable for young children. A good resource for these kinds of activities is the *Multicultural Bibliography for Preschool Through Second Grade* by Nichols and O'Neill (1977).

## COOKING

Cooking is one of the most important of all activities in a preschool curriculum because it supports growth in four developmental areas: emotional, social, intellectual, and physical development. In the area of emotional development, cooking and eating what has been cooked provide a shared classroom experience. Because the concepts of sharing with one another and working together are basic to cooking activities, the process helps children acquire concepts, skills, and knowledge related to several curriculum areas, specifically mathematics, science, social studies, and language arts. Children's physical development is promoted as they practice fine motor skills required for cutting, peeling, and slicing. Eye–hand coordination and sensory discrimination skills are also used by children as they cook.

For some children, cooking at school may be the first opportunity they have had to use cooking implements or hot plates. While it is certainly undesirable to frighten children about the dangers of cooking, it is necessary both to caution them about stoves and knives and to teach them to cook with care.

A multicultural approach to cooking has two goals: first, to encourage children to experiment with food other than that with which they are familiar and, second, to give young children a general notion of the connections between cultural heritage and the process of preparing, cooking, and eating a meal. The first goal can be met by constantly providing children with a diversity of eating and cooking experiences. The second goal can be met by presenting a variety of different ways of carrying out the process of preparing, cooking, and eating food. For example, a teacher might elect to do a short unit on breads from different cultures. As children make tortillas, cornbread, pita bread, and whole wheat bread, they are able to compare the processes and can talk about the ways in which the processes are the same and the ways in which they are different. Without giving children stereotypic information about cultures and foods, the teacher can help children to see basic connections between cooking and cultural heritage. (This unit is more appropriate for four- and five-year-olds than for three-year-olds.)

Through cooking activities children will begin to get a sense of the importance of cultural heritage and its effect on our actions. Growing, cooking, and eating food are central to all cultures. The influences of cultural heritage can be explored through a short unit, like the one on bread, which deals with the diverse uses of very similar foods in different cultures. Children can understand that people may grow the same vegetables in their gardens—corn, for example—and use them to make varied foods that are basic to their daily lives—tortillas, cornbread, polenta, cornmeal mush, spoonbread.

Habitat as well as cultural heritage, of course, greatly influences what food is grown and how it is prepared and served. While it would not be appropriate to give young children an abundance of specific information about where certain foods are grown or why some cultures cook with different spices than others, it is possible to help children understand some basic concepts about the relation of food to habitat and culture. The teacher can illustrate the influence of habitat on what people grow and eat by using developmentally appropriate examples, such as people who live by the sea and eat fish or people who have vegetable gardens and eat the corn, beans, and tomatoes they grow. Through cooking activities children are able to experience concretely the concept that there are some things that all groups of people do but that the ways in which they are done vary according to the group to which one belongs.

The recipes used can be saved to make a cookbook for the children. One might begin with recipes that include ingredients the children like to eat, such as African chicken stew with peanuts, or quesadillas, or tortillas with cheese and beans. Recipes and cooking activities should be fairly simple. It is helpful to write the directions clearly on a recipe chart, including pictures of ingredients and symbols for measurements, so that children who are beginning to learn to read can start matching pictures and words. Depending on the facilities available, however, children can prepare a cold snack or an entire hot meal.

The children's families are one of the best potential resources for recipes. Some children may have recipes that have been in their families for a long time—perhaps recipes from grandparents. Some families may not have resources for a planned meal that includes the use of recipes; for many people eating is an issue of survival rather than a sharing, family time. Thus it is important to be conscious of the role food plays in individual children's lives. Other ways of finding out what people from various cultures eat are to look in an encyclopedia or in magazines from various ethnic groups, to read stories about different cultures, and to look in cookbooks that focus on dishes cooked by a particular ethnic group.

Cooking with children provides limitless opportunities to bring a multicultural perspective to the curriculum. It offers children the opportunity to begin to broaden their taste in foods by eating dishes from a variety of ethnic cuisines. Children can also begin to make the connections between food and cultural heritage by cooking with parents of ethnically different children in the classroom.

# EVALUATING THE CLASSROOM
# ENVIRONMENT

Teachers who are attempting to develop a multicultural classroom environment will want to evaluate their progress in each of the areas discussed in this chapter. To assist them in this process, a "Multicultural Classroom Environment Checklist" is provided as appendix D. The checklist provides specific questions that the teacher should ask to rate his or her progress in each of the major curriculum areas.

# Epilogue: Beyond the Classroom _____

In the foreword to Paulo Freire's *Pedagogy of the Oppressed* (1972), Richard Shaull writes:

> There is no such thing as a *neutral* educational process. Education either functions an an instrument which is used to facilitate the integration of the younger generation into the logic of the present system and bring about conformity to it, *or* it becomes "the practice of freedom," the means by which men and women deal critically and creatively with reality and discover how to participate in the transformation of their world. (p. 15)

In many ways this book about multicultural education has been about Freire's "practice of freedom"—freedom for children to develop in a learning environment that affirms their existence both as individuals and as members of a cultural and racial group, and freedom for adults as they continue the process of ridding themselves of negative racial attitudes.

As teachers become more involved in "the practice of freedom," they will probably develop a stronger desire to become social-change agents (thus functioning at the sixth level of involvement in multicultural education). Assuming such a role widens one's focus, moving beyond the classroom and into a larger arena of action: the school and the community. Although the specifics of the teacher's work may change, the commitment to the elimination of racism remains constant.

Once we understand about the pernicious nature of institutional racism, we can never recover the comfortable position of ignorance. We have bought a one-way ticket and there is no return—we can only move forward.

# Appendices
# References
# Index

# APPENDIX A

# Bibliography
# of Multicultural Children's
# Books _____

Adler, David A. *The House on the Roof: A Sukkot Story*. Illus. by Marilyn Hirsh. New York: Bonim Books, 1976.
> An attractive picture book that explains the origin of the Sukkot, the Jewish harvest festival.

Adoff, Arnold. *Black Is Brown Is Tan*. Illus. by Emily A. McCully. New York: Harper & Row, 1973.
> A warm, funny story-poem about a racially mixed family.

Alexander, Martha. *The Story Grandmother Told*. New York: Dial Press, 1969.
> A small black girl tells her grandmother the story she would like the older woman to tell her.

Aliki. *Corn Is Maize*. New York: Crowell, 1976.
> A simple, factual book about corn: the development of it as a food source, the life cycle of the corn plant, etc.

Anderson, Lonzo. *The Day the Hurricane Happened*. Illus. by Ann Grifalconi. New York: Scribner, 1974.
> This book includes a lot of information on hurricanes. It also tells what happens to a family in the Virgin Islands when the hurricane hits.

———. *Izzard*. Illus. by Adrienne Adams. New York: Scribner, 1973.
> Jamie lives in the Virgin Islands. His pet is a lizard that he must return to nature when it grows up.

Ayer, Jacqueline. *Nu Dang and His Kite*. New York: Harcourt, 1959.
> Nu Dang is a young Siamese boy who has a very beautiful kite. When the kite floats away and Nu Dang goes hunting for it, readers see much of the country of Siam.

Baldwin, Ann Norris. *Sunflowers for Tina*. Illus. by Ann Grifalconi. New York: Four Winds, 1970.

> A young black girl who lives in an urban environment finds some flowers in an empty lot.

Balet, Jan. *The Gift, A Portugese Christmas Tale*. New York: Delacorte, 1967.

> A beautifully illustrated Christmas story about young Joanjo and his gifts for the Christ Child.

Baylor, Byrd. *Hawk, I'm Your Brother*. Illus. by Peter Parnall. New York: Scribner, 1976.

> A young boy who lives in the desert steals a baby hawk from its nest, hoping that he, too, can learn to fly.

Belpre, Pura. *Santiago*. Illus. by Symeon Shimin. New York: Warne, 1968.

> This well-illustrated picture book is the story of a young boy who moves from Puerto Rico to New York City.

Benchley, Nathaniel. *Small Wolf*. Illus. by Joan Sandin. New York: Harper & Row, 1972.

> Small Wolf, a young American Indian, sees white people for the first time and witnesses the white people's takeover of Manhattan Island.

Blood, Charles L. *The Goat in the Rug*. Illus. by Nancy Winslow. New York: Parents Magazine Press, 1976.

> The story of how Navajo rugs are made, beginning with the shearing of the goat and ending with the weaving itself.

Blue, Rose. *I Am Here: Yo estoy aqui*. Illus. by Moneta Barnett. New York: Watts, 1971.

> Luz is lonely in kindergarten because she doesn't speak English; her teacher and a Spanish-speaking aide help her start to communicate with the other children.

Bolognese, Don. *A New Day*. New York: Delacorte, 1970.

> This picture book tells the Nativity story transposed to a migrant worker's family in the southwestern United States.

Bond, Jean Carey. *A Is for Africa*. New York: Watts, 1969.

> An alphabet book with color photographs of Africa.

———. *Brown Is a Beautiful Color*. Illus. by Barbara Zuber. New York: Watts, 1969.

> A series of images from the country and the city that give warm and positive definitions or aspects of the color brown.

Bourne, Miriam Anne. *Raccoons Are for Loving*. Illus. by Marian Morton. New York: Random House, 1968.

> A picture book about a young child from an urban area who takes a school trip to the country.

Breinburg, Petronella. *Dr. Shawn*. Illus. by Errol Lloyd. New York: Crowell, 1975.

―――. *Shawn Goes to School*. Illus. by Errol Lloyd. New York: Crowell, 1973.

―――. *Shawn's Red Bike*. Illus. by Errol Lloyd. New York: Crowell, 1976.

Shawn is a young and very personable black boy whose adventures and feelings are ones with which preschool children can identify.

Brenner, Barbara. *Bodies*. New York: Dutton, 1973.

―――. *Faces*. New York: Dutton, 1970.

With minimal text and simple black-and-white photographs, Brenner shows us how alike and how varied all people are.

Burch, Robert. *Joey's Cat*. Illus. by Don Freeman. New York: Viking Press, 1969.

Joey is a young black boy whose cat has kittens; it's up to Joey to convince his mother that the kittens must come indoors for their own safety.

Caines, Jeanette Franklin. *Abby*. Illus. by Steven Kellogg. New York: Harper & Row, 1973.

Abby is a young black girl who is adopted. The story centers on her relationships with her adoptive parents and brother, Kevin.

―――. *Window Wishing*. Illus. by Kevin Brooks. New York: Harper & Row, 1980.

The story of a vacation spent by two black children with their grandmother.

Calloway, Northern J., and Hall, Carol. *Super-Vroomer!* Illus. by Sammis McLean. New York: Doubleday, 1978.

Three young black children build a box car and enter it in a race held in a predominantly white part of town.

Clifton, Lucille. *Amifika*. Illus. by Thomas DiGrazia. New York: Dutton, 1977.

A story for very young children about the father's return from the armed services.

―――. *The Boy Who Didn't Believe in Spring*. Illus. by Brinton Turkle. New York: Dutton, 1973.

Two friends, one black and one white, explore their city for the first sign of spring.

―――. *Everett Anderson's Nine Month Long*. Illus. by Ann Grifalconi. New York: Holt, Rinehart & Winston, 1978.

Everett Anderson, a young black boy, notices changes in his mother and in their home, and finds out about the baby that is about to be born.

————. *Some of the Days of Everett Anderson*. Illus. by Evaline Ness. New York: Holt, Rinehart & Winston, 1970.

> Another Everett Anderson book, this one is a collection of short poems about Everett Anderson and the city where he lives.

Cohen, Miriam. *Will I Have a Friend?* Illus. by Lillian Hoban. New York: Macmillan, 1967.

> The story of a young child's first day in kindergarten.

Coker, Gylbert. *Naptime*. New York: Delacorte, 1978.

> An almost wordless picture book about naptime in a racially balanced day-care center.

Damjan, Mischa. *Atuk*. Illus. by Gian Casty. New York: Pantheon, 1964.

> The story of the Eskimo, Atuk, and his huskie puppy.

Delaney, A. *The Butterfly*. New York: Delacorte, 1977.

> This book shows the flight of a butterfly and the children—black and white, girls and boys—who chase gleefully after it.

De Paola, Tomie. *Watch Out for the Chicken Feet in Your Soup*. Englewood Cliffs, N.J.: Prentice-Hall, 1974.

> Joey takes his friend to visit his Old World Italian grandmother and learns that his grandmother's foreign accent and cultural differences can be interesting and appreciated rather than ridiculed.

Feelings, Muriel. *Jambo Means Hello; Swahili Alphabet Book*. Illus. by Tom Feelings. New York: Dial Press, 1971.

> A lovely picture book with simple, warm text and beginning, easy phrases in Swahili.

————. *Moja Means One: Swahili Counting Book*. Illus. by Tom Feelings. New York: Dial Press, 1973.

> A beautifully illustrated counting book; the numbers from one to ten are given in English and Swahili.

————. *Zamani Goes to Market*. Illus. by Tom Feelings. New York: Seabury, 1970.

> The story of a young boy from East Africa, his first trip to market, and the present he buys for his mother.

Freeman, Don. *Corduroy*. New York: Viking Press, 1965.

> The story of a young black girl and the teddy bear, Corduroy, that she finds in a busy department store.

Garrett, Helen. *Angelo, the Naughty One*. Illus. by Leo Politi. New York: Viking Press, 1944.

> A colorful picture book set in a Mexican village. Angelo, who hates to take baths, gets in trouble on his sister's wedding day.

Goble, Paul. *The Friendly Wolf*. Scarsdale, N.Y.; Bradbury Press, 1975.

> Two Native American children, separated from their family, are befriended and helped back home by a wolf.

―――. *The Girl Who Loved Wild Horses*. Scarsdale, N.Y.: Bradbury Press, 1978.

A young Native American girl loves to ride with the wild horses—more than being with her family and tribe.

Graham, Lorenz. *Song of the Boat*. Illus. by Leo and Diane Dillon. New York: Crowell, 1975.

A West African story of a father and son and their search for a tree from which to make a canoe.

Greenfield, Eloise. *Africa Dream*. Illus. by Carole Byard. New York: John Day, 1977.

A fantasy story in which a young black girl dreams about being in Africa.

―――. *Honey I Love and Other Poems*. Illus. by Diane and Leo Dillon. New York: Crowell, 1978.

Lovely, soft illustrations combine with simple, warm poems in this book about a young black girl and the people who are a part of her life.

―――. *Me and Nessie*. Illus. by Moneta Barnett. New York: Crowell, 1975.

The picture book story of a young black girl, her family, her imaginary friend (Nessie), and her first day at school.

Grifalconi, Ann. *City Rhythms*. Indianapolis, Ind.: Bobbs-Merrill, 1975.

A young child discovers the varied rhythm and mood of the city in which he lives.

Grimes, Nikki. *Something on My Mind*. Illus. by Tom Feelings. New York: Dial Press, 1978.

A book of poems for all children about the problems of being a child in our world. The illustrations are quite beautiful.

Grossman, Barney, Groom, Gladys, and the pupils of P.S. 150, Bronx, New York. *Black Means . . .* Illus. by Charles Bible. New York: Hill & Wang, 1970.

School children offer their thoughts and feelings for positive definitions of the word *black*.

Hall, Carol, and Calloway, Northern J. *I Been There*. Illus. by Sammis McLean. New York: Doubleday, 1977.

A young boy's imaginative adventures in outer space.

Harper, Anita. *How We Live*. Illus. by Christine Roche. New York: Harper & Row, 1977.

―――. *How We Work*. Illus. by Christine Roche. New York: Harper & Row, 1977.

These colorful picture books show the many ways we live and work; many types of families and colors of people are shown.

Hill, Elizabeth Starr. *Evan's Corner*. Illus. by Nancy Grossman. New York: Holt, Rinehart & Winston, 1967.

> A crowded apartment in a busy city didn't give Evan much room for himself. This book is about how he solved the problem.

Hirsch, Marilyn. *Potato Pancakes All Around: A Hanukkah Tale*. New York: Bonim Books, 1978.

> This humorous story celebrates some of the traditions of the Jewish Hanukkah.

Hitte, Kathryn. *Mexicali Soup*. Illus. by Anne Rockwell. New York: Parents Magazine Press, 1970.

> In this Chicano family, Mama is glad to be in a big city where she can get the best ingredients for her Mexicali soup; her children, however, are embarrassed about the soup and try to get Mama to change the recipe. A humorous story, but also a lesson about trying too hard to adapt to another culture.

Howell, Ruth Rea. *A Crack in the Pavement*. Photographs by Arlene Strong. New York: Atheneum, 1970.

> A well-photographed book about things that grow in a city.

Isadora, Rachel. *Ben's Trumpet*. New York: Greenwillow Books, 1979.

> A young black child in an urban neighborhood loves the music of the trumpet player in a nearby jazz club.

Keats, Ezra Jack. *Apt. 3*. New York: Macmillan, 1971.

> Two small children explore their apartment building.

––––––. *Goggles*. New York: Macmillan, 1969.

> Two young boys outwit a gang of older boys.

––––––. *Hi Cat!* New York: Macmillan, 1972.

> Another Keats story about inner city children; this one concerns two young boys and a stray cat.

––––––. *A Letter to Amy*. New York: Harper & Row, 1968.

> Peter's birthday party would be "all boys" if it weren't for Amy.

––––––. *Pet Show!* New York: Macmillan, 1972.

> A pet show brings many kids and their pets together, even young Archie who can't find his cat to enter him in the show.

––––––. *Peter's Chair*. New York: Harper & Row, 1967.

> Peter has trouble getting used to his new role as big brother until he realizes that he has special privileges and abilities because of his age and size.

––––––. *Whistle for Willie*. New York: Viking Press, 1964.

> A beautiful picture book of a child's solitary play and beginning attempts at whistling.

Keats, Ezra Jack, and Cherr, Pat. *My Dog Is Lost*. New York: Crowell, 1960.

A bilingual picture book: Juanito is lonely in New York City, can't speak English, and has lost his dog!

Kessler, Leonard. *Last One In Is a Rotten Egg*. New York: Harper & Row, 1969.

Freddy must work to overcome his fear of the water while his friends are swimming and diving.

Krementz, Jill. *Sweet Pea: A Black Girl Growing Up in the Rural South*. New York: Harcourt, 1969.

Black-and-white photographs and ten-year-old Sweet Pea's own words tell about growing up black in the rural South.

Levitin, Sonia. *A Sound to Remember*. Illus. by Gabriel Lisowski. New York: Harcourt Brace Jovanovich, 1979.

Central to the plot of this story is the Jewish tradition of blowing the ram's horn on Rosh Hashanah.

Lexau, Joan M. *Benjie*. Illus. by Don Bolognese. New York: Dial Press, 1964.

Benjie, a shy black boy, helps his Granny find her lost earring.

———. *Benjie on His Own*. Illus. by Don Bolognese. New York: Dial Press, 1970.

When his grandmother falls ill, Benjie finds out a lot about the neighbors and their willingness to help.

———. *I Should Have Stayed in Bed*. Illus. by Syd Hoff. New York: Harper & Row, 1965.

A humorous story about a very bad day of a young black boy.

———. *Me Day*. Illus. by Robert Weaver. New York: Dial Press, 1971.

Rafer's birthday is a very special day—in spite of his anxiety about whether he will get a letter from his father. This is a good picture of a black family coping with the father's absence.

———. *The Rooftop Mystery*. Illus. by Syd Hoff. New York: Harper & Row, 1968.

A mystery story for beginning readers involving a black family's move to a new home just a few blocks from their old home.

McGovern, Ann. *Black Is Beautiful*. Photographs by Hope Wurmfield. New York: Four Winds, 1969.

A book of images—simple words and photographs—showing the beautiful and positive connotations of the word *black*.

Maiorano, Robert. *Francisco*. Illus. by Rachel Isadora. New York: Macmillan, 1978.

This story, set in the Dominican Republic, is about a young boy who finds a way to earn money and help his family.

Martin, Patricia Miles. *The Little Brown Hen*. Illus. by Harper Johnson. New York: Crowell, 1960.

A young boy, searching for his hen, finds it on a nest of young ducks. This book features a black family in a rural setting.

Matsuno, Masako. *A Pair of Red Clogs*. Illus. by Kazue Mizumura. Cleveland, Ohio: Collins-World, 1960.

A Japanese grandmother remembers her first pair of red clogs as she prepares to give her granddaughter a pair of red clogs.

Maury, Inez. *My Mother and I Are Growing Strong/Mi mama y yo nos hacemos fuertes*. Illus. by Sandy Speidel. Stanford, Calif.: New Seed, 1978.

The story of a Latino mother and daughter and how they learn to do many new things while the husband/father is in prison.

Milgram, Mary. *Brothers Are All the Same*. Photographs by Rosemarie Hausherr. New York: Dutton, 1978.

Nina, a young white girl, narrates this well-photographed story about the adoption of her darker-skinned brother.

Morrow, Suzzane Stark. *Inatuk's Friend*. Illus. by Ellen Raskin. Boston, Mass.: Little, Brown, 1968.

The story is of Inatuk, an Eskimo, who leaves his best friend behind when his family moves to a city.

Musgrove, Margaret W. *Ashanti to Zulu: African Traditions*. Illus. by Leo and Diane Dillon. New York: Dial Press, 1976.

This alphabet book illustrates some of the more exotic customs of the many nations of Africa.

Nolan, Madeena Spray. *My Daddy Don't Go to Work*. Illus. by Jim LaMarche. Minneapolis, Minn.: CarolRhoda Books, 1978.

A very good book about what happens to a young black girl and her parents when her father loses his job.

Perrine, Mary. *Salt Boy*. Illus. by Leonard Weisgard. Boston, Mass.: Houghton Mifflin, 1968.

The story of Salt Boy, a Navajo Indian, whose job it is to care for his mother's sheep; Salt Boy would rather rope and tame wild horses.

Rosario, Idalia. *Idalia's Project ABC: An Urban Alphabet Book in English and Spanish*. New York: Holt, Rinehart & Winston, 1981.

A bilingual alphabet book.

Schick, Eleanor. *One Summer Night*. New York: Greenwillow Books, 1977.

Laura starts dancing in her room one hot summer night, and before long her entire neighborhood—an urban, ethnically diverse community—is celebrating in a spontaneous party.

Schweitzer, Byrd Baylor. *Amigo*. Illus. by Garth Williams. New York: Macmillan, 1963.

This book is about a young boy and a prairie dog who "tame" each other in spite of strong advice to the contrary from both families.

Scott, Ann H. *On Mother's Lap*. Illus. by Glo Coalson. New York: McGraw-Hill, 1972.

In this Eskimo family, the young boy is concerned that his mother's lap might not be big enough for him and his infant sister.

———. *Sam*. Illus. by Symeon Shimin. New York: McGraw-Hill, 1967.

The story of a young black boy, Sam, and his very busy family.

Simon, Norma. *All Kinds of Families*. Chicago: Albert Whitman, 1975.

This book shows the diversity of life-styles and families people have.

———. *I'm Busy, Too*. Illus. by Dora Leder. Chicago: Albert Whitman, 1980.

A warm and realistic story about three children in a multiracial day-care center.

Solbert, Ronni. *I Wrote My Name on the Wall*. Boston, Mass.: Little, Brown, 1971.

A photographic adventure in a large multiethnic city.

Sonneborn, Ruth A. *Friday Night Is Papa Night*. Illus. by Emily A. McCully. New York: Viking Press, 1970.

A Spanish-speaking family anxiously awaits the father's return at the end of the week; the father's work takes him away from his wife and children from Monday to Friday.

———. *I Love Gram*. Illus. by Leo Carty. New York: Viking Press, 1971.

A young girl, her working mother, and her active grandmother are the triple heroines of this picture book.

Steptoe, John. *Stevie*. New York: Harper & Row, 1969.

The young boy resents the boarder the family took in, until the boarder leaves.

Stone, Elberta. *I'm Glad I'm Me*. Illus. by Margery W. Brown. New York: Putnam, 1971.

This young black child considers many things he might be before coming to a positive statement about himself.

Surowiecki, Sandra Lucas. *Joshua's Day*. Chapel Hill, N.C.: Lollipop Power, 1972.

Joshua is a young boy who lives with his mother, attends a multiracial day-care center, and has some exasperating experiences there on one particular day.

Sutherland, Efua. *Playtime in Africa*. Illus. by Willis Bell. New York: Atheneum, 1962.

Clear, simple photographs and text show African children at play.

Thomas, Ianthe, *Hi, Mrs. Mallory!* Illus. by Ann Toulmin-Rothe. New York: Harper & Row, 1979.

The friendship between an elderly white woman and a young black girl is the basis of this book.

————. *Walk Home Tired, Billy Jenkins*. Illus. by Thomas DiGrazia. New York: Harper & Row, 1974.

>Billy and his sister have a long walk through an inner city neighborhood to get to their home, and Billy is tired. His sister's fantasies and stories help make the walk a true adventure.

Topping, Audrey. *A Day on a Chinese Commune*. New York: Grosset & Dunlap, 1972.

>Through the simple text and photographs, readers learn about life on a Chinese commune.

Uchida, Yoshiko. *The Birthday Visitor*. Illus. by Charles Robinson. New York: Scribner, 1975.

>Emi, a Japanese-American girl, is going to be seven and is not pleased to have a visitor from Japan to share that special day.

————. *The Forever Christmas Tree*. Illus. by Kazue Mizumura. New York: Scribner, 1963.

>This picture book is a Christmas story set in Japan.

————. *The Rooster Who Understood Japanese*. Illus. by Charles Robinson. New York: Scribner, 1976.

>This beautifully illustrated picture book is about a Japanese-American family and their bilingual menagerie, including a chicken named Mr. Lincoln.

Udry, Janice May. *Mary Jo's Grandmother*. Illus. by Eleanor Mill. Chicago: Albert Whitman, 1970.

>The story of Mary Jo's visits to her grandmother, who lives alone out in the country. During one visit Mary Jo must go out in the snow for help when her grandmother falls and injures her leg.

————. *What Mary Jo Shared*. Illus. by Eleanor Mill. Chicago: Albert Whitman, 1966.

>Mary Jo has a hard time deciding what to share with her class during "show and tell."

Vogel, Ray. *The Other City*. New York: David White, 1969.

>Four high school students talk about and photograph their section of Brooklyn.

Ward, Leila. *I Am Eyes/Ni Macho*. Illus. by Nonny Hogrogian. New York: Greenwillow Books, 1978.

>A beautifully illustrated book about the early morning as seen by a young child in Kenya.

Wyse, Anne, ed. *Alphabet Book*. Toronto, Canada: University of Toronto, 1969.

>Illustrated in black and white, this alphabet book deals with the lives of Native Americans living in Ontario, Canada.

Yarbrough, Camille. *Cornrows*. Illus. by Carole Byard. New York: Coward, McCann & Geoghegan, 1979.

During "storytellin' time," when the children must sit still and have their hair braided, the mother and great-grandmother tell about the history of "cornrowing," or braiding hair, in African culture.

Yashima, Taro. *Crow Boy*. New York: Viking Press, 1955.

A young boy from the mountain area of Japan goes into a village to school and must gain the friendship of the other students.

———. *Seashore Story*. New York: Viking Press, 1967.

A beautiful picture book and folk tale from Japan.

———. *Umbrella*. New York: Viking Press, 1958.

A story about a very young Japanese girl who is just learning to walk.

# APPENDIX B

## Bibliography on Institutional Racism

Alford, Harold J. *The Proud Peoples: The Heritage and Culture of Spanish-Speaking People in the United States*. New York: New American Library, 1973.

> This book discusses the contributions of Spanish-speaking peoples to the history of the United States.

Allport, Gordon W. *The Nature of Prejudice*. Garden City, N.Y.: Anchor–Doubleday, 1958.

> The author discusses the origins of prejudice, its many expressions in society, and how it affects people.

Bennett, Lerone. *Before the Mayflower: A History of the Negro in America*. Chicago: Johnson, 1969.

> This is a startling history of black contributions to the development of the United States.

Bidol, Patricia. *Mini-Lecture: Difference Between Prejudice and Racism*. Detroit: People Acting for Change Together, n.d.

> This is a basic work in which the author gives clear, concise definitions of racism and prejudice and discusses both the terms and their effects on contemporary American culture.

———. *Reflections of Whiteness in a White Racist Society*. Detroit: People Acting for Change Together, n.d.

> The author discusses thoroughly what it means to be white in contemporary American society.

Brown, Dee. *Bury My Heart at Wounded Knee*. New York: Holt, Rinehart & Winston, 1970.

> This is a landmark book that tells—from an Indian perspective—about white people's destruction of American Indian civilization and culture.

Cade, Toni, ed. *The Black Woman*. New York: New American Library, 1970.

This is a collection of essays on black women in contemporary America.

Carter, Thomas P. *Mexican Americans in School: A History of Educational Neglect*. New York: College Entrance Examination Board, 1970.

This is a report of a thorough study of Mexican-American children in the southwestern United States.

Chapman, Abraham, ed. *Black Voices: An Anthology of Afro-American Literature*. New York: New American Library, 1968.

A well-organized collection of literature by eminent black writers such as Langston Hughes, Richard Wright, and Arna Bontemps.

Citron, Abraham F. *The 'Rightness of Whiteness'—The World of the White Child in a Segregated Society*. Detroit: Wayne State University, College of Education, Office of Urban Education, 1971.

In this pamphlet, the author discusses the cultural deprivation of white children and the effect of racism on them.

Clark, Kenneth B. *Dark Ghetto*. New York: Harper & Row, 1965.

The author discusses the social and political power structure of Harlem in the 1960s and profiles important figures in the Civil Rights Movement.

Coles, Robert. *Children of Crisis*. Boston, Mass.: Little, Brown, 1967.

A fascinating study of black children who integrated Southern schools, this work has already become a classic.

Daniels, Roger, and Kitano, Harry H. *American Racism: Exploration of the Nature of Prejudice*. Englewood Cliffs, N.J.: Prentice-Hall, 1970.

This comprehensive look at racism and prejudice draws the reader's attention to the pattern of racial prejudice and the various racial groups and cultures that have suffered from it.

Ellison, Ralph. *Invisible Man*. New York: New American Library, 1952.

This is the human condition reduced to race relations. It is a story of a black man's search for identity. Winner of the National Book Award for fiction.

Franklin, John Hope. *From Slavery to Freedom*. New York: Knopf, 1967.

An important history of black culture and the struggle against racism in North America.

Freire, Paulo. *Pedagogy of the Oppressed*. New York: Herder & Herder, 1970.

Freire addresses issues such as oppressors and oppressed, education as a tool of oppression, and liberation: a "mutual process." This book is essential for educators who are interested in education as an instrument for liberation.

Goodman, Mary Ellen. *Race Awareness in Young Children*. New York: Collier, 1964.

> The author reports on several studies on children's race awareness and suggests that children learn racial differences and negative attitudes at a very early age.

Gossett, Thomas F. *Race: The History of an Idea in America*. New York: Schocken Books, 1965.

> The author traces the history and development of the concept of race from ancient cultures through colonial America to the present.

Grier, William H., and Cobbs, Price M. *Black Rage*. New York: Grove, 1967.

> Two black psychiatrists discuss in very clear and concise language some of the essential problems that exist between black and white people.

Haley, Alex, ed. *Autobiography of Malcom X*. New York: Grove, 1967.

> The gripping story of one of the most powerful men in the Black Revolution. The book played a major part in the consciousness raising of white America regarding the seriousness of black people's demands.

Harrington, Michael. *The Other America*. New York: Macmillan, 1962.

> A basic study of poverty in America. Of particular interest here is chap. 4, pt. 3: "If you're Black, stay back."

Hessel, Dieter T., and Perry, Everett, eds. *The White Problem*. New York: Presbyterian Distribution Service, 1970.

> An action guide for people who want to work against racism.

Jones, James M. *Prejudice and Racism*. Reading, Mass.: Addison-Wesley, 1972.

> A complete treatment of prejudice and racism with respect to contemporary American society.

Josephy, Alvin M., ed. *Red Power: The American Indian Fight for Freedom*. New York: McGraw-Hill, 1971.

> A collection of articles about the struggle of American Indians for equality.

Katz, Judy H. *White Awareness: Handbook for Anti-Racism Training*. Norman: University of Oklahoma Press, 1978.

> This book is a practical guide with many resources.

Katz, Phyllis A., ed. *Towards the Elimination of Racism*. New York: Pergamon Press, 1976.

> An exhaustive review of current literature on race attitudes and behavior change. Much of the book is devoted to research on children's racial awareness and attitudes.

Kitano, Harry H. *Japanese Americans*. Englewood Cliffs, N.J.: Prentice-Hall, 1976.

The author reviews the history of Japanese-Americans in this country and discusses the effect of such events as their wartime internment.

Knowles, Louis, and Prewitt, Kenneth, eds. *Institutional Racism in America*. Englewood Cliffs, N.J.: Prentice-Hall, 1969.

A very clear and concise presentation of the pervasiveness of institutional racism.

Kovel, Joel. *White Racism: A Psychohistory*. New York: Pantheon, 1970.

The author discusses racism as a pathological factor in our society and postulates some radical changes necessary to eradicate it.

Lerner, Gerda, ed. *Black Women in White America*. New York: Vintage Books, 1973.

A unique collection of documents: letters, statements, articles, manuscripts, written by American women, mostly black, from 1870 to 1970.

McWilliams, Carey. *North from Mexico: The Spanish-Speaking People of the United States*. Westport, Conn.: Greenwood Press, 1968.

The author discusses the cultural heritage of, the discrimination against, and the political activism of Mexican-Americans in the United States.

Schwartz, Barry N., and Disch, Robert. *White Racism: Its History, Pathology and Practice*. New York: Dell, 1970.

A comprehensive collection of articles, essays, and excerpts on the many facets of racism.

Sedlacek, William E., and Brooks, Glenwood C. *Racism in American Education: A Model for Change*. Chicago: Nelson-Hall, 1976.

The authors provide a step-by-step program for combatting racism in education.

Silberman, Charles E. *Crisis in Black and White*. New York: Random House, 1964.

The author discusses the heavy toll racial oppression takes on black people in our society.

————. *Crisis in the Classroom: The Remaking of American Education*. New York: Random House, 1970.

The author analyzes in very concrete terms the failures of the American educational system and discusses future directions and remedies.

Simmen, Edward, ed. *Pain and Promise: The Chicano Today*. New York: New American Library, 1972.

A collection of essays about the Chicano reactions to and methods of dealing with oppression by white society.

Smith, Lillian. *Killers of the Dream*. New York: W. W. Norton, 1949.

Lillian Smith is a white woman who grew up in the South. She writes, in this autobiography, about the racism in the South and its effect on her.

Sue, Stanley, and Wagner, Nathaniel, eds. *Asian Americans: Psychological Perspectives*. Palo Alto, Calif.: Science and Behavior, 1973.

> A group of articles that discusses Asian-Americans in contemporary culture in the United States.

Sung, B. L. *The Story of the Chinese in America*. New York: Macmillan, 1974.

> A thorough study of Chinese in the United States, including the history of oppression Chinese-Americans have suffered.

Terry, Robert W. *For Whites Only*. Grand Rapids, Mich.: William B. Eerdmans, 1970.

> The author discusses what white people can do to work against institutional racism.

United Church of Christ. *Racism/Sexism: A Resource Packet for Leaders*. St. Lcuis, Mo.: DECEE [United Church of Christ, Division of Evangelism, Church Extension and Education], 1979.

> "A new resource for leaders . . . who want to study the relationship between racism and sexism, and who want to analyze their effects on individual lives and the institutions of American and global society" (Introduction).

U.S. Commission on Civil Rights. *Racism in America and How to Combat It*. Washington, D.C.: Clearinghouse Publications, Urban Series No. 1, 1970.

> This report discusses racism in all areas of American society and the barriers that work against racial equality.

Valdez, Luis, and Steiner, Stan, eds. *Aztlan, An Anthology of Mexican American Literature*. New York: Knopf, 1972.

> The editors have included both historical and present-day selections in this fine anthology of writings by Mexican-Americans.

Vivo, Paquita. *The Puerto Ricans: An Annotated Bibliography*. New York: Bowker, 1973.

> An extensive, annotated bibliography on Puerto Ricans and Puerto Rico, written in English.

Witt, Shirley, and Steiner, Stan, eds. *The Way, An Anthology of American Indian Literature*. New York: Knopf, 1972.

> This anthology, a collection of Native American writings, includes sections on the white people's takeover of Native American land, on the new Indian, and on education and culture, among other subjects.

Woodward, C. Vann. *The Strange Career of Jim Crow*. 3rd rev. ed. New York: Oxford University Press, 1974.

> A clear and concise account of segregation in the southern United States from 1877 to the present.

Young, Whitney M. *Beyond Racism*. New York: McGraw-Hill, 1969.
The author discusses common misunderstandings about race and America's racial problems and puts forth a program for racial equality.

# APPENDIX C

## Sources
## for Multicultural
## Materials ————————————————————

## AIDS FOR MULTICULTURAL
## CURRICULUM DEVELOPMENT

American Association of Colleges for Teacher Education, Commission on Multicultural Education. *No One Model American* . . . Washington, D.C.: American Association of Colleges for Teacher Education, 1972.

American Library Association Task Force on Ethnic Materials Exchange. *Multi-Ethnic Media: Selected Bibliographies in Print*. Chicago: American Library Association, 1976.

Buttlar, Lois, and Wynar, Lubomyr. *Building Ethnic Collections: An Annotated Guide for School Media Centers and Public Libraries*. Littleton, Colo.: Libraries Unlimited, 1977.

Chambers, Dewey W. *Children's Literature in the Curriculum*. Chicago: Rand McNally, 1971.

Crosby, Muriel, ed. *Reading Ladders for Human Relations*. Washington, D.C.: American Council on Education, 1963.

*Cultural Diversity in Early Childhood Education Teacher Training Manual*. San Francisco: St. Patrick's Day Care Center (366 Clementina St.), 1978.

Flemming, Bonnie Mack, Hamilton, Darlene, and Hicks, Jo Anne. *Resources for Creative Teaching in Early Childhood Education*. New York: Harcourt Brace Jovanovich, 1977.

Griffin, Louise, compiler. *Multi-Ethnic Books for Young Children*. Washington, D.C.: National Association for the Education of Young Children, 1970.

*Interracial Books for Children Bulletin*. New York: Council on Interracial Books for Children, 1966–present.

Johnson, Harry A., ed. *Ethnic American Minorities: A Guide to Media and Materials*. New York: Bowker, 1976.

Katz, Lucinda Lee, compiler. *Bilingual/Bicultural/Multicultural Resources*. Urbana: ERIC/University of Illinois, 1974.

Lass-Woodfin, Mary Jo. *Selected Books on American Indians*. Chicago: American Library Association, 1977.

McNeill, Earldene, Allen, Judy, and Schmidt, Velma. *Cultural Awareness for Young Children*. Dallas: Learning Tree, 1975.

Mills, Joyce, ed. *The Black World in Literature for Children: A Bibliography of Print and Nonprint Materials*. Atlanta: Atlanta University School of Library Science, 1975.

Rollins, Charlamae, ed. *We Build Together*. Champaign, Ill.: National Council of Teachers of English, 1967.

Rollock, Barbara, compiler. *The Black Experience in Children's Books*. New York: New York Public Library, 1974.

Seattle Public School District No. 1. *Rainbow ABC's*. Huntington Beach, Calif.: Creative Teaching Press, n.d.

Seattle Public School District No. 1. *Rainbow Activities Book*. Huntington Beach, Calif.: Creative Teaching Press, n.d.

Van Why, Elizabeth W., compiler. *Adoption Bibliography and Multi-Ethnic Sourcebook*. West Hartland, Conn.: Open Door Society of Connecticut, 1977.

Weinberg, Meyer, compiler. *The Education of the Minority Child: A Comprehensive Bibliography of 10,000 Selected Entries*. Chicago: Integrated Education Associates, n.d.

Wisconsin Department of Public Instruction. *Starting Out Right: Choosing Books About Black People for Young Children, Preschool Through Third Grade*. Washington, D.C.: Day Care and Child Development Council of America, n.d.

Wolf-Wasserman, Miriam, and Hutchinson, Linda. *Teaching Human Dignity: Social Change Lessons for Everyteacher*. Minneapolis: Education Exploration Center, 1979.

## RESOURCE CENTERS FOR MULTICULTURAL MATERIALS[1]

American Indian Project
San Francisco Unified School District
135 Van Ness Avenue, Room 19
San Francisco, CA 94102

---

[1]This list is taken in part from Bonnie Mack Flemming and Darlene Softley Hamilton, *Resources for Creative Teaching in Early Childhood Education* (orig. *Songs and Parodies* by Joanne Deal Hicks) (New York: Harcourt Brace Jovanovich, 1977), p. 113. Reprinted with permission.

Anti-Defamation League of B'nai B'rith
823 United Nations Plaza
New York, NY 10017

Appalachia Educational Laboratory
1031 Quarier Street
P.O. Box 1348
Charleston, WV 25325

Association on American Indian Affairs
432 Park Avenue South
New York, NY 10016

Black Child Development Institute
1463 Rhode Island Avenue, N.W.
Washington, D.C. 20005

Bureau of Curriculum Innovation
Massachusetts Department of Education
182 Tremont Street
Boston, MA 02111

Community Change, Inc.
P.O. Box 146
Reading, MA 01867

Council on Interracial Books for Children (CIBC)
1841 Broadway
New York, NY 10023

Far West Laboratory for Educational Research and Development
1855 Folsom Street
San Francisco, CA 94103

Japanese American Curriculum Project, Inc.
414 East Third Street
P.O. Box 367
San Mateo, CA 94401

Mexican American Cultural Center
3019 West French Place
San Antonio, TX 78228

Multicultural Resources Center
c/o Margaret S. Nichols or Peggy O'Neill
P.O. Box 2945
Stanford, CA 94305

National Educational Laboratory Publishers, Inc.
P.O. Box 1003
Austin, TX 78767

Navaho Curriculum Center
Rough Rock Demonstration School
Chinle, AZ 86503

People Acting for Change Together (PACT)
163 Madison
Detroit, MI 48226

Presbyterian Distribution Service
475 Riverside Drive
New York, NY 10027

R and E Research Associates
936 Industrial Avenue
Palo Alto, CA 94303

United Church of Christ
Division of Evangelism, Church Extension and Education
Box 179
St. Louis, MO 63166

U.S. Committee for UNICEF
331 East Thirty-eighth Street
New York, NY 10016

Women's Action Alliance
370 Lexington Avenue
New York, NY 10017

# APPENDIX D

# Multicultural
# Classroom Environment
# Checklist _____

This checklist is designed to help teachers determine if education that is multicultural is going on in the classroom. By using the checklist, the teacher will focus on individual aspects of the classroom environment and curriculum, highlighting areas of the curriculum that need improvement. Teachers are encouraged to rate the classroom environment as it is currently, not as they would like it to be.

## LANGUAGE ARTS

1. Does the classroom have a wide variety of age-appropriate and culturally diverse books and language arts materials?

    Yes _____    No _____

2. Are there stories about persons from each of the following cultural groups in the book corner?

    _____ Native American     _____ Spanish-speaking
    _____ Asian-American      _____ black
    _____ a variety of white ethnic groups

3. Are there any books that speak of people of diverse cultures in stereotypic or derogatory terms (for example, describing black people as lazy or Native Americans as "savage") that should be removed from the collection?

    Yes _____    No _____

4. Are the pictures of people on the walls and on the bulletin boards representative of a multicultural community?

  Yes _____ No _____

## SOCIAL STUDIES

5. Does the curriculum as a whole help children increase their understanding and acceptance of attitudes, values, and life-styles that are unfamiliar to them? If so, how?

  Yes _____ No _____

6. Are materials and games racially or sex role stereotypic—for example, are Native Americans pictured in tepees and called "Little Red" or "brave"? Are women depicted only as care givers while men do lots of exciting jobs?

  Yes _____ No _____

## BLOCKS

7. Are the accessories in the block area representative of various cultural groups and family configurations?

  Yes _____ No _____

8. Are the people block accessories stereotypic in terms of sex roles?

  Yes _____ No _____

## DRAMATIC PLAY

9. Is there a wide variety of clothes, including garments from various cultural groups, in the dramatic play area?

  Yes _____ No _____

10. Are the pictures on the walls and the props in the dramatic play area representative of a diversity of cultures?

  Yes _____ No _____

11. Are the dolls in the dramatic play area multiracial?

  Yes _____ No _____

12. Are the brown, red, yellow, and black dolls just white dolls whose skin color has been changed?

    Yes _____    No _____

## MUSIC AND GAMES

13. Do the music experiences in the curriculum reinforce children's affirmation of cultural diversity?

    Yes _____    No _____

14. Are finger plays, games, and songs from various cultural groups used in the classroom?

    Yes _____    No _____

## COOKING

15. Do the cooking experiences in the classroom encourage children to experiment with foods other than those with which they are familiar?

    Yes _____    No _____

16. Are the cooking experiences designed to give young children a general notion of the connections between cultural heritage and the process of preparing, cooking, and eating food? If so, how?

    Yes _____    No _____

# References _____

Almy, M., & Genishi, C. *Ways of studying children* (Rev. ed.). New York: Teachers College Press, 1979.

Banks, J. A. (Ed.). *Teaching ethnic studies: Concepts and strategies* (Forty-third Yearbook of the National Council for the Social Studies). Washington, D. C.: National Council for the Social Studies, 1973.

Beuf, A. *Red children in white America.* Philadelphia: University of Pennsylvania Press, 1977.

Biber, B. A developmental-interaction approach: Bank Street College of Education. In M. C. Day & R. K. Parker (Eds.), *The preschool in action: Exploring early childhood programs* (2nd ed.). Boston: Allyn & Bacon, 1977.

Biber, B., Shapiro, E., & Wickens, D. *Promoting cognitive growth.* Washington, D.C.: National Association for the Education of Young Children, 1971.

Bruner, J. Nature and uses of immaturity. In J. Bruner, A. Jolly, & K. Sylvia (Eds.), *Play: Its role in development and evolution.* New York: Basic Books, 1976.

Burgest, D. R. The racist use of the English language. *The Black Scholar*, 1973, *5*, 37–45.

Chesler, M. A. Teacher training designs for improving instruction in interracial classrooms. *Journal of Applied Behavioral Science*, 1971, *7*, 612–41.

————. *What happened after you desegregated the white school?* Atlanta: Southern Regional Council, Inc., 1967.

Citron, A. *The 'rightness' of 'whiteness'—The world of the white child in a segregated society.* Detroit: Wayne State University, College of Education, Office of Urban Education, 1971.

Clark, D. H. *The psychology of education.* New York: Collier-Macmillan, 1967.

Cohen, D. H., & Stern, V. *Observing and recording the behavior of young children* (3rd ed.). New York: Teachers College Press, 1983.

Cole, M. *The cultural context of learning and thinking.* New York: Basic Books, 1971.

Davidson, H. H., & Lang, G. Children's perceptions of their teachers' feelings toward them related to self-perception, school achievement, and behavior. *Journal of Experimental Education*, 1960, *29*, 107–18.

Derman-Sparks, L., Higa, C. T., & Sparks, B. Children, race, and racism: How race awareness develops. *Interracial Books for Children Bulletin*, 1980, *11* (3–4), 3–9.

Dolce, C. Multicultural education—some issues. *Journal of Teacher Education*, 1973, *24*, 282–84.

Flemming, B. M., Hamilton, D. S., & Hicks, J. D. *Resources for creative teaching in early childhood education*. New York: Harcourt Brace Jovanovich, 1977.

Freire, P. *Pedagogy of the oppressed*. New York: Herder & Herder, 1970.

Gay, G. Racism in America: Imperatives for teaching ethnic studies. In J. A. Banks (Ed.), *Teaching ethnic studies: Concepts and strategies* (Forty-third Yearbook of the National Council for the Social Studies). Washington, D.C.: National Council for the Social Studies, 1973.

Ginsburg, H., & Opper, S. *Piaget's theory of intellectual development* (2nd ed.). Englewood Cliffs, N.J.: Prentice-Hall, 1979.

Gold, M. J., Grant, C. A., & Rivlin, H. N. (Eds.). *In praise of diversity: A resource book for multicultural education*. Washington, D.C.: Teacher Corps and Association of Teacher Educators, 1977.

Goodman, M. E. *Race awareness in young children*. Cambridge, Mass.: Addison-Wesley, 1952; 2nd ed., New York: Crowell-Collier, 1964.

Grant, C., & Grant, G. The multicultural evaluation of some second and third grade textbook readers—A survey analysis. *Journal of Negro Education*, 1981, *50*, 63–74.

Hirsch, E. (Ed.). *The block book*. Washington, D.C.: National Association for the Education of Young Children, 1974.

Holt, J. *How children fail* (rev. ed.). New York: Dell, 1982.

Hovey, E. *Ethnicity and early education*. Urbana, Ill.: ERIC Clearinghouse on Early Childhood Education, 1975. (ERIC Document Reproduction Service No. ED 107 368).

John, V. P. Styles of learning—styles of teaching: Reflections on the education of Navajo children. In C. B. Cazden, V. P. John, & D. Hymes (Ed.), *Functions of language in the classroom*. New York: Teachers College Press, 1972.

Kamii, C., & DeVries, R. *Group games in early education*. Washington, D. C.: National Association for the Education of Young Children, 1980.

Katz, J. H. *White awareness*. Norman: University of Oklahoma Press, 1978.

Katz, P. A. (Ed.). *Towards the elimination of racism*. New York: Pergamon Press, 1976.

Kuroiwa, P. The "invisible students." *Momentum*, 1975, *6*, 34–36.

Longstreet, W. S. Learning and diversity: The ethnic factor. *Educational Research Quarterly*, 1978, *2*, 60–73.

Mercer, J. *SOMPA technical manual*. New York: The Psychology Corporation, 1979.

Mitchell, L. S. *Young geographers*. New York: Bank Street College, 1971.

Morris, J. B. Indirect influences on children's racial attitudes. *Educational Leadership*, 1981, *38*, 286–87.

Nichols, M. S., & O'Neill, M. N. *Multicultural bibliography for preschool through second grade: In the areas of Black, Spanish-speaking, Asian American, and Native American cultures*. Stanford: Multicultural Resources, 1977.

Opie, I., & Opie, P. *Children's games in street and playground*. London: Oxford University Press, 1969.

Porter, J. *Black child, white child: The development of racial attitudes*. Cambridge, Mass.: Harvard University Press, 1971.

Pushkin, I., & Veness, T. The development of racial awareness and prejudice in children. In P. Watson (Ed.), *Psychology and race*. Chicago: Aldine, 1974.

Ramsey, P. G. Beyond "Ten Little Indians" and turkeys—Alternative approaches to Thanksgiving. *Young Children*, 1979, *34*, 28–32, 49–52.

*Random House Dictionary*, unabridged edition. New York: Random House, 1978.

Riessman, F. Styles of learning. *NEA Journal*, 1966, *55*, 15–17.

Rollins, C. (Ed.). *We build together*. Champaign, Ill.: National Council of Teachers of English, 1967.

Shapiro, E., & Biber, B. The education of young children: A developmental-interaction approach. *Teachers College Record*, 1972, *74*, 55–79.

Sprung, B. *Non-sexist education for young children*. New York: Citation Press, 1975.

Stabler, J. R., & Jordan, S. A. The measurement of children's self-concept as related to racial membership. *Child Development*, 1971, *42*, 2094–97.

Stone, L. J., & Church, J. *Childhood and adolescence* (3rd ed.). New York: Random House, 1973.

Subtle racism seen in North. *Durham Morning Herald*, May 18, 1978, p. 2.

Taba, H. *Curriculum development: Theory and practice*. New York: Harcourt Brace Jovanovich, 1962.

———. *With perspectives on human relations*. Washington, D.C.: American Council on Education, 1955.

Taba, H., Durkin, M. C., Fraenkel, J. K., & McNaughton, A. H. *A teacher's handbook to elementary social studies* (2nd ed.). Reading, Mass.: Addison-Wesley, 1971.

U.S. Commission on Civil Rights. *Racism in America and how to combat it*. Washington, D. C.: Clearinghouse Publications, Urban Series No. 1, 1970.

U.S. Equal Employment Opportunity Commission. *Employment opportunity in the schools*. Washington, D.C.: Government Printing Office, 1977, 1978.

Werner, E. E., Bierman, J. M., & French, F. E. *The children of Kauai*. Honolulu: University of Hawaii Press, 1971.

*Who Am I?* New York: Scholastic Magazine, 1972. (Filmstrip)

Williams, J. E., & Morland, J. K. *Race, color, and the young child*. Chapel Hill: University of North Carolina Press, 1976.

Wilson, G. The word nigger is what's not allowed. *Interracial Books for Children Bulletin*, 1980a, *11* (3–4), 16–18.

Wilson, G. (Ed.). Children, race and racism: How race awareness develops. *Interracial Books for Children Bulletin*, 1980b, *11* (3–4).

Youngblood, C. E. Multicultural early childhood education. *Viewpoints in teaching and learning*, 1979, *55*, 37–43.

# Index ──────────────────────────────────────

Ability grouping, 25
Almy, M., 14
Asian-American children, 15

Banks, J. A., 3
Bannerman, Helen, 60
Behavioral patterns, 18
Beuf, A., 19
"Beyond 'Ten Little Indians' and Turkeys" (Ramsey), 54
Biber, B., 1, 6
Bierman, J. M., 14
Block play, 64–66
Books: children's, 61
*Brown* v. *Board of Education* (U.S. Supreme Court, 1954), 2
Bruner, Jerome, 9
Burgest, D. R., 24

Chesler, M. A., 24; quoted, 4
Child development: learning styles in, 12–19; philosophies of, 6; preschool, 7–12; racial awareness and attitudes in, 19–21
*Children's Games in Street and Playground* (Opie), 71
Church, J., quoted, 8, 9
Citron, A., 21
Clark, D. H., 12
Classroom environment. *See* Learning environment
Cohen, D. H., 14
Cole, M., 13

Community: monocultural v. multicultural, 3
Cooking, 52, 72–74
Cultural diversity: positive aspects of, 7
Culture: defined, 13
Curriculum: aids for multicultural development of, 98 99; checklist for classroom environment, 102–04; cooking, 72–74; dramatic play, 67–69; guidelines, 32–35; language arts, 58–62; and levels of involvement, 36–40; multicultural materials and activities in, 24, 41–57; music and games, 69–72; preschool, 30; priorities, 24; social studies, 62–64; unit blocks as part of the, 64–66

Davidson, H. H., 5
Derman-Sparks, L., 20, 33
Development: defined, 6
Developmental-interaction philosophy, 1, 6–7
Dialect: in children's books, 61
Discrimination: defined, 23
Dolce, C., quoted, 3
Dolls, 68
Dramatic play, 67–69
Durkin, M. C., 42

*Ebony* (periodical), 62
Education, multicultural: approach to, 2, 4; goals of, 3; levels of involvement in, 36–40; parents' reaction to, 27–29; preschool, 9; theoretical basis for, 30–32
Egocentrism, 8–9

*Essence* (periodical), 62
Ethnicity: defined, 13; learning styles and, 12–15
Ethnocentrism, 1, 7, 9
Evaluation process, 56–57

Flemming, B. M., 53
Folk songs, 69
Folk tales, 62
Folkways Records, 69
Fraenkel, J. K., 42
Freire, Paulo, 76
French, F. E., 14

Games, 71–72
Gay, G., 3
Genishi, C., 14
Ginsburg, H., 8, 10
Gold, M. J., 3
Goodman, M. E., 20, 33
Grant, C., 24
Grant, C. A., 3
Grant, G., 24

Hamilton, D. S., 53
Hicks, J. D., 53
Higa, C. T., 20, 33
Hirsch, E., 64
Hispanic children, 14
Holidays, 53
Holt, J., 25
Hovey, E., 14
Human relations, education for, 1, 6–7

IQ tests, 24
Interaction: defined, 6

*Jet* (periodical), 62
John, Vera P., 14
Jordan, S. A., 21

Katz, J. H., 25
Katz, P. A., 20, 21
Keats, Ezra Jack, 61
Kuroiwa, P., 15

Lang, G., 5
Language arts, 58–62
Learning environment, 6; activities, 44–56, 63; checklist, 102–04; interaction in, 15–19; multicultural, 39, 41–44, 58–75;
    racial and ethnic composition, 2, 39; and the teacher's role, 1–2, 4, 18, 27–29
Learning styles, 12–19
*Little Black Sambo* (Bannerman), 60
Longstreet, Wilma S., 16, 18; quoted, 13

Magazines, ethnic, 62
Map making, 65
McNaughton, A. H., 42
Mercer, J., quoted, 24
Mitchell, Lucy Sprague, 65
Morland, J. K., 20
Morris, J. B., 20, 33; quoted 21
*Multicultural Bibliography for Preschool Through Second Grade* (Nichols, O'Neill), 72
Music, 53, 69–70

*National Geographic Magazine*, 62
Navajo children, 14
Nichols, M. S., 72
*Non-Sexist Education for Young Children* (Sprung), 68

*Observing and Recording the Behavior of Young Children* (Cohen, Stern), 14
O'Neill, M. N., 72
Opie, Iona, quoted, 71
Opie, Peter, quoted, 71
Opper, S., 8, 10

Parents: multicultural attitudes of, 27–29
*Pedagogy of the Oppressed* (Freire), 76
People block accessories, 66
Piaget, Jean, 8
Play, patterns of, 9–10
Poems, 62
Porter, J., 20, 21
Pratt, Caroline, 64
Prejudice: defined, 23
Preschool children: development of, 7–12
Problem solving, 10–12
Pushkin, I., 19

Racial attitudes, 2–3, 19–27
Racial slurs, 35
Racism: cultural, 24, 61; defined, 23; individual, 23; institutional, 2
Ramsey, Patricia G., 54
Resource centers for multicultural materials, 99–101

*Resources for Creative Teaching in Early Childhood Education* (Flemming, Hamilton, Hicks), 53
Riessman, F., quoted, 16
Rivlin, H. N., 3
Role models, 1–2, 25, 63
Rollins, Charlamae, 61
Routines, daily, 54

School boards, 4
Shapiro, E., 1, 6
Shaull, Richard, quoted, 76
*Snowy Day, The* (Keats), 61
Social studies, 62–64
Sources for multicultural materials, 98–101
Sparks, B., 20, 33
Sprung, B., 68; quoted, 64
Stabler, J. R., 21
Stern, V., 14
Stone, L. J., quoted, 8, 9
"Subtle Racism Seen," 2

Taba, Hilda, 1, 6–7, 42; quoted, 30
Talking together, 54

Teachers: racial attitudes of, 4–5, 22–27, 32–35; role of, 1–2, 4, 18, 27–29; as social change agents, 39–40
Time, perception of, 14
Tracking system. *See* Ability grouping
"Transductive thinking," 10

Unit blocks, 64–66

Veness, T., 19
Vocabulary: racism in, 61

*Ways of Studying Children* (Almy, Genishi), 14
*We Build Together* (Rollins), 61
Wechsler Intelligence Scale for Children—Revised (WISC-R), 24
Werner, E. E., 14
Wickens, D., 6
Williams, J. E., 20
Wilson, G., quoted, 35

*Young Geographers* (Mitchell), 65
Youngblood, C. E., 3, 4